THE KNICKERBOCKER TRADITION:

Washington Irving's New York

"Diedrich Knickerbocker" by famed illustrator F.O.C. Darley (1822–1888), done for a special illustrated edition of Knickerbocker's *History of New York* after its appearance in 1848, revised, as Vol. I of the Author's Revised Edition of Irving's *Works*. From the Library of Sleepy Hollow Restorations.

THE KNICKERBOCKER TRADITION: WASHINGTON IRVING'S NEW YORK

Edited by Andrew B. Myers

SLEEPY HOLLOW RESTORATIONS

TARRYTOWN · NEW YORK

Library of Congress Cataloging in Publication Data
Main entry under title:
The Knickerbocker tradition:
Essays presented at a conference sponsored by
Sleepy Hollow Restorations, Inc.
in Tarrytown, N.Y., Oct. 28, 1972.
Bibliography: p.
1. New York (City)—History—1775–1865—Congresses.
2. New York (State)—History—1775–1865—Congresses.
3. Irving, Washington, 1783–1859—Congresses.
I. Myers, Andrew B., ed.
II. Sleepy Hollow Restorations, Tarrytown, N.Y.
III. Title.
F128.44.K54   917.47′03′3   74-678
ISBN 0-912882-08-5

For information, address the publisher:
Sleepy Hollow Restorations, Inc.
Tarrytown, New York 10591

ISBN 0-912882-08-5
Library of Congress Catalog Card Number: 74-678

First Printing

Printed in The United States of America
Designed by Ray Freiman

CONTENTS

ILLUSTRATIONS

Introduction

Andrew B. Myers

Knickerbocker is a famous name. Strictly speaking, it denotes the Dutch inheritance important to New York City, New York State, all the Middle States, and indeed the nation. In its wider sense, the Knickerbocker tradition is as broad and deep as the breeches of Governor Wouter Van Twiller of New Netherland, who was "exactly five feet six inches in height, and six feet five inches in circumference." The quotation is from Washington Irving's masterpiece of comic history, Diedrich Knickerbocker's *A History of New York* (1809), which originated "Knickerbocker" as a word evoking the essence of metropolitan New York—the city and the centuries of American history it has influenced.

The Knickerbocker tradition, seen from almost any angle, applies initially to the Hudson River Valley of colonial and early national times; but it is principally connected to the original Dutch New Amsterdam, founded in 1625 and the heart of New Netherland, and to the "New York" it became after surrender to British forces in 1664.[1] The process of change and growth in this city's long and dramatic history can still be examined with benefit as, to borrow the title of Arthur M. Schlesinger's influential book, one of our most direct paths to the present.[2]

No urban center in this country is more characteristically American in its major difficulties than metropolitan New York, and therefore more obviously a target for sharpshooting critics. At the same time New York's real and continuing successes, like its legendary skyscrapers, are equally obvious. Famous or infamous, this turbulent and powerful city stands as unique, and what is often overlooked, it has long been so. The problems which the city and its supportive suburbs (even in western Connecticut

1

and northern New Jersey) now confront, as public institutions
and as people, are not so overwhelmingly new and different that
the history and traditions of an older, and at least equally storied, New York cannot offer useful cautions and honest comfort.

"Father Knickerbocker's" New York is protean, and ever has
been so, witness, if nothing else, the nicknames it has attracted
and survived. A recent contribution—"Fun City"—is already
outdated. At the turn of this century, O. Henry's "Bagdad-
on-the-Subway" was both funny and fitting, but today seems
as old-fashioned as the first underground steam cars. He (William Sidney Porter) had better luck with "Little old New York's
good enough for us—that's what they sing," from his tale "A
Tempered Wind," for this helped perpetuate the first words as a
sentimental label.[3] Walt Whitman, in a poem dated 1860, opted
for the Indian "Mannahatta":

> *I was asking for something specific and perfect for my city,*
> *Whereupon lo! upsprang the aboriginal name.*[4]

Alas, so poetic a usage could not fit without strain the upcoming
and appallingly prosaic New York City of post-Civil War Tammany Hall, including the villainous Tweed Ring. It is worth noting in passing that the last words of Washington Irving's *History*
in 1809 were a similar salute, from the fictitious Diedrich, to his
"beloved island of Manna-hata!" The actual author retained
this closing through each of his subsequent revisions. Assuredly
it spoke for him too. As for the state, already acclaimed the Em-
pire State in his final years, it held his affections too, those of a
seasoned vacationer, and traveled native son, but to a lesser degree.

Again, on substitute names, it may also have been Irving,
even before the *History*, who in the group-authored series of
essays, etc., that in a belated eighteenth-century fashion of satirical chit-chat comprised *Salmagundi* (1807–08), supplied another shibboleth for his city in Part XVII (source unidentified),
"Of The Chronicles Of The Renowned And Ancient City Of
Gotham." The last word here has served handily as a synonym

despite the echoes of its parent nursery rhyme. Bayrd Still used it in 1956 in the kaleidoscopic *Mirror For Gotham.*[5] John Paul Pritchard was rather more the academician in 1963 with *Literary Wise Men of Gotham.*[6]

If any one term has stayed in the forefront, it is "Knickerbocker," and this includes parallel appearances of the avuncular, if not absolutely paternal, "Father" K., complete with buckled shoes, smallclothes, tie-wig, and tricorn hat. Case in point: the title chosen in 1954 by Director R. W. G. Vail for his *Knickerbocker Holiday, a Sesqui-Centennial History of the New-York Historical Society, 1804–1954.*[7] Etymologists and attendant lexicographers explain the term "Knickerbocker" as referring to New Yorkers in general, but most directly to those descended from pioneering Dutch stock. Though Washington Irving's precise source for the choice of this name is not entirely settled (a source, that is, other than the uncharted imagination), it is a fact that, early on, he did know members of settled families of that surname in the Albany and surrounding area.

There are, to be sure, two sides to this Knickerbocker coin—a Dutch profile, and another more cosmopolitan. In one view, for both the student of our immediate postrevolutionary history as well as the student of our early national literature, "Knickerbocker" is a quite familiar term, covering the fluid characteristics of a Hudson River Valley society that both in town and country was gradually leaving behind its multiform Dutch colonial heritage. The emphasis here, in a cultural sense, is on loss. This extended tradition is one way reflected in the immortal "Rip Van Winkle" tale, as its feckless hero's nameless Kaatskill "village of great antiquity" switches its allegiance and flag. Old Rip returns to find Nicholas Vedder's inn, once "designated by a rubicund portrait of His Majesty George the Third," has become "the Union Hotel, by Jonathan Doolittle," its swinging sign now displaying "GENERAL WASHINGTON." This fancifully documents a kind of pre-Kickerbocker period, if one thinks of the expression as being born about 1809. At the same time it reminds us of the transforming experience of the Revolution, which was more soberly described by the modern historian

Thomas Jefferson Wertenbaker in *Father Knickerbocker Rebels*, his title employing a readily acceptable anachronism.[8]

Other aspects of this side of the Knickerbocker tradition, however dated, can be seen in the following quotation from the poet William Cullen Bryant (1794–1878), taken from a memorial address in 1860 after Irving's death. By now also a Knickerbocker fixture, especially as editor and proprietor of New York's *Evening Post*, a leading journal for decades, Bryant was originally a New Englander who arrived only in 1825. As he speaks of Irving's faraway boyhood, his own reminiscences add a further Knickerbocker dimension:

> With the exception of the little corner of the island below the present City Hall, the rural character of the whole region was unchanged, and the fresh air of the country entered New York at every street. The town at that time contained a mingled population, drawn from different countries; but the descendants of the old Dutch settlers formed a large proportion of the inhabitants, and these preserved many of their peculiar customs, and had not ceased to use the speech of their ancestors at their firesides. Many of them lived in the quaint old houses, built of small yellow bricks from Holland, with their notched gable-ends on the streets, which have since been swept away with the language of those who built them.
>
> In the surrounding country, along its rivers and beside its harbors, and in many parts far inland, the original character of the Dutch settlements was still less changed. Here they read their Bibles and said their prayers and listened to sermons in the ancestral tongue. Remains of this language yet linger in a few neighborhoods; but in most, the common schools, and the irruptions of the Yankee race, and the growth of a population derived from Europe, have stifled the ancient utterances of New Amsterdam. I remember that twenty years since the market people of Bergen chattered Dutch in the steamers which brought them in the early morning to New York. I remember also that, about ten years before, there were families in the westernmost towns of Massachusetts where Dutch was

still the household tongue, and matrons of the English stock, marrying into them, were laughed at for speaking it so badly.[9]

Visible signs like many of these remained fixed in Irving's mind for life, but such realities did not dissuade him from vivid romanticizing when he came, as a first-generation American, to write the *History*. In 1968 *American Heritage* published a special, richly illustrated issue, "New York, N. Y.", a salute to three and a half centuries of the great city's life. One article, by Henry S. F. Cooper, Jr., the great-great-grandson of the novelist, was on Irving's indelible contribution, and was called "The Man Who Invented Dutch New York." One can guess this label was chosen tongue-in-cheek, but it does point up the combination of fact and fiction in Irving's humorous handling of his chronicles of transplanted Hollanders. Still, as Bryant reveals, the artifacts and accents derived from such Lowlands forefathers were noticeable enough even as the republic reached its first half century. Thereafter time (with the "i" standing for both immigration and intermarriage) took its remorseless toll.

And this is the other side of the coin—the cosmopolitan image. There was a new New York every long generation, not just another edition in Dutch. Almost from the start, even before the Netherlands lost sovereignty, the postage stamp of a port had an uncommonly mixed population, including slaves. Seventeenth-century Manhattan Island, and the larger of the eastward Long Island and northerly Hudson River Valley villages it simultaneously ruled and served, were heterogeneous. This gave a special spirit to this patchquilt of frontier life on the seashore and inland. In many ways this was the archetypal American experience. Crèvecoeur, whose New York State adventures included farming in upcountry Orange County, could well have been drawing on such personal contacts there when, attempting in 1782 to answer his own question of "What is an American?" he wrote, "I could point out to you a family whose grandfather was an Englishman, whose wife was Dutch, whose son married a French woman, and whose present four sons have now four

wives of different nations." This too is part of the variable
Knickerbocker tradition.[10]

The historian Carl Bridenbaugh, in *Cities in the Wilderness,*
has made much, and rightly, of the importance of the part
played by colonial towns, especially seaboard centers, "in the
transit of civilization from Europe to America."[11] The daily life
of the crucible city, *in potentia,* at the wide mouth of the Hudson, is everywhere illustrative of this concept. Cosmopolitan it
was, as metropolitan it would become. The emphasis here is on
gain.

One such gain was to be in the fine arts—albeit adolescent
New York was not yet rival to London or Paris. And the catalyst
which stimulated was material progress, in a Manhattan that in
effect was a marketplace. Already Wall Street meant dollars as
once it meant defense. The literary critic Kendall Taft, in the
anthology *Minor Knickerbockers,* has put this new influence
thus:

> At least part of New York's literary pre-eminence during the
> second, third, and fourth decades of the nineteenth century
> was a result of its physical growth and rapid mercantile prog-
> ress. Early in the century its varied opportunities began to at-
> tract ambitious young men. As time went on and the city de-
> veloped, it became increasingly true that almost all literary
> roads led to New York. Until the late thirties, when Boston for
> a time regained the ascendancy, the bustling seaport on Man-
> hattan Island was the Mecca sought by poets, playwrights,
> novelists, and other writers.[12]

The young Irving's New York was something like the young
Joyce's Dublin, a port city on an important river, a sometime
capital, and so compact one could easily walk from one end to
the other. The comparison cannot be more closely pressed, for
Manhattan had more exceptional inner resources as well as better luck. Dublin (ca. 1900) turned inward, quintessentially provincial; New York (ca. 1800) opened to the world. Almost from
its unpromising foundation as a neglected outpost of interconti-

nental rivalries New York had another destiny. Nonetheless there is a further likeness to attend. Both crowded places developed a quite distinctive local character, both in the pace of life and the oddities of common parlance, especially in a characteristic use of language. These in turn not only gave to but took from commerce, politics, and the intensities of religion. The result, as often in literature, in communities busy enough to have multiple and conflicting interests and at the same time small enough for many inhabitants to know a bit about most others, was a flourishing of easygoing wit, democratic self-criticism, and cauterizing satire. In Joyce's young manhood one result was the extraordinary Irish Renaissance; in Irving's, the so-called Knickerbocker School emerged, with himself to become the dean of the faculty.

For the struggling indigenous American world of words this concentration of talent, with an occasional touch of genius, amounted to the first solid professional success of its kind. Admittedly it was only forerunner to the spectacular midcentury American Renaissance, so often tied to Boston-cum-Cambridge-cum-Concord, and headlining Emerson, Hawthorne, and Thoreau. Let it quickly be noted that two other major figures shared the same spotlight, each a New Yorker who served an apprenticeship in later Knickerbocker journalism or letters—Herman Melville and Walt Whitman. As for the first Knickerbocker alumni, Irving's name remains fresh, and certainly Cooper's, though Bryant's has faded to a degree. Over the three or four decades of coherently Knickerbocker performance in prose and verse, lesser figures, like James Kirke Paulding, John Howard Payne, and Nathaniel Parker Willis, came and went. Much more important, Edgar Allan Poe ventured onto the Manhattan scene during the 1830s and 1840s, suffering in the end an outrageous fortune, in feuds that were almost epidemic, in what Perry Miller has called, although perhaps too melodramatically, New York's "literary butcher shop."[13]

Yet literary influence as such was far from all Knickerbocker New York could boast of, as the intimate and extensive diaries of prominent figures like Philip Hone (Mayor in 1825) and midcentury attorney George Templeton Strong reveal. Authorship is only one possible example of the expanding energies of native or adopted sons and daughters. Even the "original" Knickerbocker world of author-about-town Washington Irving was never its artistic expression alone, any more than, say, the imperial Athens of Pericles was Greek tragedy and little else, or that, to jump milleniums, the Chicago that Carl Sandburg celebrated was stockyards and little else. The hungry reach of the city often exceeded its grasp, in countless directions; still it kept reaching. By Irving's valetudinarian years in the 1850s his comparatively puny birthplace had become a colossus for its time, for one thing with a larger population, almost a million, than that of the entire state in 1783. Its traditions now included leadership in the nation as well.

James Fenimore Cooper (1794–1851) at his death left unfinished a historical work apparently to be called "The Towns of Manhattan," an enthusiastic examination of the actual and potential of the powerful city he had long known well, despite extended family residence in upstate Cooperstown. His description widens and deepens New York's influence for now it "is essentially national in interests, position, and pursuits. No one thinks of the place as belonging to a particular state, but to the United States."[14]

No one? Here in the heyday of P. T. Barnum this is excusable hyperbole, though one can believe a rigorously honest Cooper considered it a veritable fact. But, soaring ambitions and fluctuating mundane values aside, Cooper's much complimented and envied "Manhattanese towns" still had outspoken local pride, old families as well as new (with concomitant problems) and a strong awareness of their own precise place on the map. In the same years in which the fabled novelist was reflecting on this more kingsize than Knickerbocker subject, Irving was applying himself, for the thriving New York City firm of George P. Putnam, to the business of an Author's Revised Edition of all his works, a multivolumed project (1848–51) that was to become the first viable venture of its kind, economic as well as aesthetic, in the young history of American publishing. When reworking *A History of New York* for inclusion, Irving dwelt in a preface on the genesis and reputation of his comic master-piece. His conclusion, dated "Sunnyside, 1848" attests to the amazing vitality of the "Knickerbocker" name, now become a tradition—a constant in a city so driven to change.

I dwell on this head, because, at the first appearance of my work, its aim and drift were misapprehended by some of the descendants of the Dutch worthies; and because I understand that now and then one may still be found to regard it with a captious eye. The far greater part, however, I have reason to flatter myself, receive my good-humored picturings in the same temper with which they were executed; and when I find, after a lapse of nearly forty years, this hap-hazard pro-duction of my youth still cherished among them; when I find its very name become a "household word," and used to give the home stamp to everything recommended for popular ac-ceptation, such as Knickerbocker societies, Knickerbocker in-surance companies, Knickerbocker steamboats, Knickerbocker omnibuses, Knickerbocker bread, and Knickerbocker ice; and when I find New-Yorkers of Dutch descent priding themselves upon being "genuine Knickerbockers," I please myself with the persuasion that I have struck the right chord; that my dealings with the good old Dutch times; and the customs and usages derived from them, are in harmony with the feelings and humors of my townsmen; that I have opened a vein of pleasant associations and quaint characteristics peculiar to my native place, and which its inhabitants will not willingly suffer to pass away; and that, though other histories of New-York may appear of higher claims to learned acceptation, and may take their dignified and appropriate rank in the family li-brary, Knickerbocker's history will still be received with good-humored indulgence and be thumbed and chuckled over by the family fireside.[15]

These autobiographical remarks by Irving end on a domestic and nostalgic note, one fitting enough for an aging author contemplating the surprising activity of an overgrown brainchild, but they are tangential to a subsequent researcher's more analytical line of approach. Like "Jeffersonian" or "Jacksonian" in our cultural evolution, an admittedly more circumscribed "Knickerbocker tradition" is also both one thing and many. Even the quotation above makes clear that Knickerbocker both denotes and connotes. Precise definition thus remains a puzzle, and indeed may not be indispensable for present purposes.

To be sure, Knickerbocker as a recognizable symbol can still be used simply enough, and regularly is, all these generations later, in advertising and in athletics, among other local enterprises. But as a clarifying concept in the study of multitudinous American experience, especially urban, it may be best to continue to handle it loosely. There have been, after all, many Knickerbocker worlds, beginning with Washington Irving's imaginary New Amsterdam and then, as actual history, extending forward to our own times of civil rights crises, conurbation, sharp church-and-state differences of opinion, etc.

This volume gathers selected nineteenth-century elements— political, social, and literary—of this plainly epic story. First, Michael D'Innocenzo of Hofstra University discusses "The Popularization of Politics in Irving's New York," investigating specifics of political practices and patterns in the very years in which, as a gentleman amateur, Irving was daydreaming of and scribbling vigorously away at Knickerbocker's *History*. Next, James F. Richardson of the University of Akron, and a native New Yorker, widens the lens in "New York Society: High and Low" to produce vivid pictures of social classes and conflicts in later Knickerbocker generations, by which time Irving had become a fondly regarded first citizen.

Joseph L. Blau of Columbia University, a distinguished scholar in the history of religious thought in America, moves in a sense from the City of Man to the City of God with his essay, "Religion and Politics in Knickerbocker Times." His interpretation of sensitive problems inherent in the relations of churches and governments necessarily expands the discussion from city to statewide affairs.

Turning to literary themes, Michael L. Black of Bernard M. Baruch College of the City University of New York analyzes "Political Satire in Knickerbocker's *History*," clarifying the sources and targets of Irving's pointed jibes. Then the editor describes the progress of Washington Irving's home in "Sunnyside: From Saltbox to Snuggery to Shrine," tracing the visits of the famous and aspiring and the simply curious to Irving's home. Finally, Jacob Judd of Herbert H. Lehman College of the City University of New York contributes an overview of this period, called "New York: A City of Constant Change and Accommodation."

These themes are of interest as examples of earlier challenge and response in a New York community that even then could be too quick-spirited and colorful for us to hope to catch its elusive mercury in any but a collective flask like this.

The Popularization of Politics
in Irving's New York

Michael D'Innocenzo

NEW YORK'S political campaigns in the early nineteenth century were volatile and bitter.[1] A Rhode Island newspaper observed that, "Electioneering in New-York is conducted with
greater acrimony and zeal that we have ever known exhibited in
any other state."[2] The election of 1807 was especially contentious because the key prize of the governorship was at stake.
This triennial quest for the state's highest office prompted extraordinary political efforts. Federalists, hoping that 1807 would
mark their return to power, were even willing to take the expedient path of backing the discredited Republican, Governor
Morgan Lewis, who had been their opponent in the previous contest. This was also the election in which 24-year-old Washington
Irving campaigned vigorously for the New York City Federalist
ticket. When it became clear that his efforts had gone for a los-
ing cause, Irving wrote to a young woman friend:

> I got fairly down into the vortex, and before the third day
> was expired, I was as deep in mud and politics as ever a mod-
> erate gentleman would wish to be; and I drank beer with the
> multitude; and I talked handbill-fashion with the dema-
> gogues, and I shook hands with the mob—whom my heart
> abhorreth. . . . Oh, my friend, I have been in such holes and
> corners; such filthy nooks and filthy corners. . . . I shall not be
> able to bear the smell of beer or tobacco for a month to
> come.[3]

Washington Irving soon elaborated on his electioneering experience in one of the *Salmagundi* essays (1807–08). He de-

scribed American politics as "a pure unadulterated 'logocracy,' or government of words."[4] In a passage which might have been written by a Twain or a Mencken, Irving asserted:

> I almost shrink at the recollection of the scenes of confusion, of licentious disorganization which I have witnessed during the last three days. I have beheld this whole city, nay, this whole State, given up to the tongue and the pen; to the puffers, the bawlers, the babblers, and the slang-whangers. I have beheld the community convulsed with a civil war, or civil talk; individuals verbally massacred, families annihilated by the whole sheetfuls, and slang-whangers cooly bathing their pens in ink and rioting in the slaughter of their thousands. I have seen, in short, that awful despot, the people, in the moment of unlimited power, wielding newspapers in one hand, and with the other scattering mud and filth about, like some desperate lunatic relieved from the restraints of his strait-waistcoat. . . . I have seen liberty; I have seen equality; I have seen fraternity!—I have seen that great political puppet-show—*an election*.[5]

That Irving's satire was true to the mark is confirmed by politcal activists of his time. Just prior to the 1807 election, Hudson Valley Federalist Charles Foote warned that "the craftsmen of democracy" would be ever ready "to furnish the means of success, to dress up old naked stories, to patch those which begin to be out at the elbows, and to enlist new ones. Lies of all descriptions from the light coloured fib, down to the copper–faced brimstone perjury, are beginning to be as plentiful as counterfeit banknotes."[6]

Disparaging views of New York elections were not limited to one party. (Antifederalist forces in both state and nation had appellations. They referred to themselves as Democrats, Republicans and Democratic-Republicans, often using the terms interchangeably.) The Democratic-Republicans leveled charges against the Federalists which sounded very much like their opponents' own complaints. Republican leaders warned that the state would soon "be overrun with their expresses and messengers [and] deluged with their handbills and pamphlets. No expense will be spared; no intrigue will be omitted; no falsehood will be overlooked. Every engine of alarm and terror; every art of seduction and intrigue . . . will be exerted."[7]

Between 1800 and 1816 Federalists and Democratic-Republicans exhibited significant similarities in their electioneering practices. In New York, at least, Federalists tended to be an exception to some of Shaw Livermore's conclusions in *The Twilight of Federalism*. They did use patronage for party needs; they did subsidize party newspapers; they systematically printed and distributed pamphlets and handbills; they took voters to the polls; and they attempted to "jolly-up" prospective voters with libations and/or money.[8]

In his splendid volume, *The Revolution of American Conservatism*, David Hackett Fischer argues that a generation gap among Federalists prompted younger men "to create popularly oriented vote seeking political organizations which might defeat Jefferson with his own weapons."[9] He further suggests that because the young Federalists offered intense, partisan competition, they stimulated an extraordinary surge of voter participation; and, in so doing, they contributed to significant changes in the structure of society and politics.[10] Fischer's essay is brilliantly provocative. He acknowledges, however, that the comprehensive, national scope of his study should raise more questions than it answers. It is my intention to focus on one aspect of this subject, the nature and effects of electioneering practices in New York. Moreover, because of obvious limitations of space, I will often refer to the election of 1807—the one that so briskly involved Washington Irving—as representative of the political activity of this period.

Both New York parties relied heavily upon county correspondence committees and public meetings to develop platforms and to campaign for candidates.[11] The "numerous and respectable" freeholders and voters usually played a role of endorsing rather than initiating action at these "managed" meetings.[12] Federalists seem to have been as concerned as Republicans about distribut-

"Tammany Hall in 1830," the lower Manhattan headquarters of the "Society of Tammany, or Columbian Order," founded c. 1783, formally organized 1789. This potent Democratic party organization offered Washington Irving its nomination for Mayor of New York in 1838. Characteristically he declined. From Rufus Rockwell Wilson, *New York: Old & New*, Vol. I. (Philadelphia, 1903).

ing circulars and handbills.[13] This means of appealing to voters was important because newspapers were relatively expensive and extremely partisan.[14]

Each party endeavored to balance its tickets with the hope of satisfying different geographical areas and attracting particular religious, nationality, or occupational groups.[15] Republicans appealed to people of German nationality in their own language in 1800 and Federalists complained that they lost over 100 votes in the 7th ward of New York City because of this tactic. The Republicans' success in that election was also attributed to their use of "carriages, chairs, and wagons, constantly going and coming, bring up to the poll every man in their interest, who could be found within 12 miles."[16] A Federalist commentator concluded that his party should have assessed these circumstances more realistically, and employed similar tactics. Indeed, it was not long before the Republicans were complaining about Federalist resourcefulness at the polls, particularly the manipulation of black voters. In the hotly contested election of 1807, Federalists were charged with buying black votes and with delivering Negroes to the polls in coaches.[17] These tactics evidently had long-range results. After the 1813 election, Republicans charged that "people of color" in New York City again voted almost exclusively for the Federalists, were responsible for carrying their ticket, and gave them a majority in the assembly. According to the *Albany Argus*, here was "the first instance on record in this country, of the political complexion of a house . . . being decided by *negro votes*."[18] (When New York's suffrage laws were rewritten at the constitutional convention of 1821, Bucktails, as the Republicans were called, remembered Negro partisanship, and they limited the voting rights of blacks.)

The support of New York City's cartmen, mechanics, mariners, and shoemakers was explicitly sought by both parties. Federalist newspapers invited cartmen to political meetings and printed their party testimonials.[19] If the Republican papers are to be believed, Federalist city officials also threatened to refuse renewal of cartmen's licenses unless they voted the right way.[20] Republicans also sought the support of the mechanics, especially by persuading them that the Federalists regarded them in a condescending manner.[21] A favored technique was to print an address to the mechanics from a mechanic:

> We mechanics and plain men are never noticed by federalists except at and about election. One would suppose that the oculist had at these times performed an operation on their eyes, for on all other occasions, they pass us as if they were purblind and could not see far off. But now, who so complaisant? They can see, and bow the head, and sometimes go so far as to shake us by the hand.[22]

Shoemakers were another special interest group whose votes were sought as a bloc. Federalists complained that in 1800 "means were found to enlist a body of the shoemakers, to the number of six or seven hundred" in opposition to them.[23] In subsequent years, and especially in 1807, they charged that the independence of the mechanics in general and the shoemakers in particular had been undermined by the Republicans' support of prison workshops.[24] The New York *American Citizen* denied the allegations, and expressed confidence that "Shoemakers and Mechanics in general . . . have too much sense and spirit to be duped by the artifices of the federal party."[25]

Religious appeals were commonplace with both parties. Federalists made particular efforts to win the support of Quakers in 1807.[26] But the greatest battles for the favor of religious groups focused on the Irish Catholics. Federalists lamented the extent to which the Irish were mobilized to vote for their opponents. The country, they complained, was "destined to be ruled by foreigners." The Republicans' actions in naturalizing and using immigrants to control elections "ought to make the blood of every American boil in his veins."[27] In 1807 the *Evening Post* accused the Hibernian Provident Society of political partisanship on behalf of the Republicans, and of forming a "JACOBIN CLUB" which excluded from membership anyone known to vote for the Federalist ticket. Complain as they did about "an organized body of foreigners," the Federalists prudently sought to garner votes by appealing "to the Irish People who Have Become Adopted Citizens of America."[28] The Irish were warned that Democrats would seek to "dupe" them by saying "a great deal about republican principles, and the sovereignty of the people; and when they get your suffrages, treat you with sovereign contempt."[29]

The Democratic press made especially vigorous appeals to the Irish in 1806 and 1807.[30] They queried: How could "Rufus King and the British Party" be supported in America when the Irish in Ireland had been tortured and massacred by the British? Catholics were reminded that "A TORY is a TORY all the world over. In the abuse and persecution of your religion here by FEDERALISTS, you see the principles and the cruelty of the BRITISH GOVERNMENT."[31] It was not coincidental that the strongest appeals were made on the final two election days of 1807. The Irish were told that Lewis and the Federalists regarded them as criminals, drunkards, rioters, and vagabonds. The *American Citizen* concluded: "Is there an Irishman in this city who after reading the above can vote for the federal party, or for a *single man* upon that ticket?"[32]

The *Evening Post* sought to deflate the Republicans by accusing them of insulting Catholics during their Sunday worship by "scandalously distributing electioneering handbills at your Church door, and by sticking them upon the pillars of your place of worship."[33] Republicans retaliated by charging the Federalists with putting a Catholic on their ticket merely as a lure for Irish votes.[34] The *American Citizen* later gloated over the failure of this tactic, and emphasized that this sole Federalist, Catholic nominee received 140 votes fewer than the lowest candidate for that party. The conclusion seemed obvious—even when a Catholic was being used by their party, regular Federalist voters could not bring themselves to support him.[35]

Not surprisingly, both parties resorted to smear tactics, especially in applying the "Tory" label to each other. The experience of the Revolution continued to be significant in the political consciousness of the voters. It was accentuated, no doubt, by the international conditions of the times. Each party made particular efforts to show that it had been on the Whig side. Both used the old soldier of '76 appeal to woo voters—even better was the old wounded soldier of '76.[36]

The Republicans urged electors in 1800 to stand with the men who "stood forward and opposed arbitrary principles in the year 1776," and to reject the Federalist ticket, which included one Loyalist and others, who, if not Loyalists, were "next of kin."[37] Federalists grew weary of such attacks, and claimed that the "cry in favor of the 'men of 1776' [was] hollow and insincere," and was only used by Republicans "to get power and place [while] laughing in their sleeves at the credulous fools who are the dupes of their cunning tricks."[38] But the bloody flag of '76 continued to be waved more than four decades after the Revolution. In the spirited 1807 election, Democrats not only accused Federalists of using a phony carpenter to appeal to the city mechanics, but they also claimed that the man was a Tory.[39] This sparked a series of charges and countercharges as to "Which is the Tory Ticket?"[40]

Federalists and Republicans alike devoted much time to electioneering. Their efforts ranged from extensive correspondence to spending days riding through one or more counties. Final election day activities could prompt men to rise at 3 A.M.[41] Federalist Robert Troup said he was so busy during one election that he didn't get to sit down from 7 A.M. to 7 P.M., or to eat dinner for three days.[42] Some political leaders were so concerned about campaigning that they even declined to run for office because they felt restricted by the etiquette expected of candidates. One Federalist emphasized that he would have greater electioneering freedom and could "do more" for the party "by being at liberty than tonguetied as a candidate."[43]

The reputation and character of a candidate were electioneering issues. Daniel D. Tompkins was belittled by Federalists in 1807 because he was the son of a farmer. But his own supporters proudly affirmed that "both the father and the son have followed the plough."[44] After two terms as governor, Tompkins was still being defended against charges that he didn't have the proper family status to be governor.[45] An indication of the changing role of candidates can probably be gleaned by this contemporary comment on "The Farmer's Boy" or "Plow Boy Dan": " 'He had the faculty . . . of never forgetting the name or face of any person with whom he had once conversed; of becoming acquainted and appearing to take an interest in the concerns of their families; and of securing, by his affability and amiable address, the good opinion of the female sex, who, although possessed of no vote, often exercise a powerful indirect influence.' "[46]

One of the more unusual character indictments was made against Thomas Grosvenor, a Federalist of Columbia County, in 1809. Grosvenor was charged with promoting a billiards game between "Mr. B.," a skillful, but "somewhat intoxicated" player, and a young man who knew little about the game. Grosvenor bet on the young man and agreed to pay the experienced "Mr. B." all that he might win. According to an electioneering broadside:

> As soon as Mr. B. was engaged in playing, Mr. Grosvenor left the room and went to the dwelling of Mr. B. not far distant. This was about eleven o'clock at night. He entered the bedchamber of Mrs. B. who was asleep; undressed himself, and got into bed to her. Being about the size of Mr. B. he intended to have imposed himself on Mrs. B. as her husband. Mrs. B. fortunately discovered the imposture immediately on his getting into bed, and by her cries, awakened a family then residing in a different part of the same house. When Mr. Grosvenor found himself detected, he made haste to escape. . . .[47]

The writer of this account said that Grosvenor could be identified by the clothes he left behind. The broadside concludes: "Had he succeeded in his hellish purpose, he would have doomed an amiable, innocent and virtuous woman to perpetual misery. . . . And now this monster in iniquity claims the public confidence."

The parties seemed equally resourceful in using unethical or illegal tactics to influence voters. These ranged from threats of

job dismissals,[48] to handing out rigged ballots, to outright bribery. The absence of official ballots gave party workers ample opportunities to employ imaginative techniques. It was clearly desirable to have the last word with a voter prior to an election.
Federalists revealed the Republicans' strategy in the 6th and 7th
wards from a conversation they purportedly overheard: " 'There
is not one half of these two wards who can read a ticket, and
those who attack them last are sure to get their votes . . . besides
I can buy half their votes for a drink of grog a man—they are a
pretty set to be sure; but they answer our purpose; and that is
all we care about them.' "[49]

The Republicans reversed the charges in the next election.
Federalists were accused of plying voters "with a strong glass of
grog," forcing tickets into the hands of cartmen, and then "seize
that hand (sic) with their own, and thus handcuffed like, lead
them up to the very ballot box without quitting their hold, or
allowing them to look at or examine the ticket."[50]

Ballot trickery was bipartisan. Republicans distributed to
Federalist voters senate tickets which contained the wrong first
name of the Federalist candidate. Voters thought they were getting their preferred ticket, but the incorrect first name invali-
dated the ballot.[51] Democratic-Republican campaigners were
also charged with distributing ballots that placed four or five of
their own assembly candidates' names in the middle of a Federal list.[52] In 1807, the Federalists were accused of using the
same tactic.[53]

Charges of outright bribery and partisanship by election
inspectors were frequently exchanged.[54] The 1807 election again
serves as an example. Affidavits were printed stating that Federalists offered to pay cartmen two dollars and to give them as
much as they could eat and drink if they voted their ticket.[55] The
Republicans complained in the same election that Federalists
planned to disrupt the 7th ward election in New York City by
the use of their "committee of interruption," which would seek
to cause commotion, and to obstruct and retard the voting process. Federalist inspector Stuyvesant was also accused of "wan-
tonly procrastinating" the election by challenging so many vot-

ers, and by "creating a pernicious delay."[56] He was further charged with accepting all Federalist tickets without question because they could be identified by "a private red mark upon them."[57]

Federalists answered that their inspectors were determined to fulfill their legal responsibilities. They noted that in some counties inspectors "were driven from the polls and severely beaten" by Republicans. The result was that four times the eligible voters cast ballots.[58] Federalists vigorously defended their inspectorial vigilance in the 6th and 7th wards because Irishmen were trying to vote with false naturalization certificates. The *Evening Post* sought to intimidate aliens prior to the election by warning them that the penalty for voting without being properly naturalized was *"Four Years in the State Prison."* Yet, the *Post* lamented after the polling that aliens who presented naturalization certificates could not legally be barred from voting.[59] Federalists bitterly complained that more than 1,900 Irish had been naturalized within four months in order to qualify them as voters. They emphasized that ancient republics had fallen because of the "bringing in of foreigners, by ambitious and selfish demagogues, to overrule the native citizens."[60]

During the next gubernatorial election (1810), Federalists protested that Republicans were arranging the transfer of deeds in some counties to qualify males of legal age for the suffrage. The Albany Corresponding Committee implored its fellow Federalists: "This practice must be met as far as it can be legally by correspondent exertions."[61] They evidently took effective action, because Martin Van Buren was soon complaining that the Federalists were outdistancing the Democrats in "fagot [transferred] holdings."[62]

Although both parties had similar electioneering practices, the Federalists often expressed a more negative or condescending view of the masses and of democracy, particularly in their private letters.[63] Ebenezer Foote's Federalist correspondents minced no words: "The *people* are *corrupt* and with as much (with perhaps even more) ease influenced to wrong as to *right*.

. . . The people in mass must have less to do with affairs or we shall perish."[64] Others complained about the suffrage being too widespread, about the "flood of democracy," the "baneful notions of Gallic phrenzy," and the "irresistible Fury" when "the Demon of Democracy rages."[65] Federalists lamented that when the Democrats acted in "the name of the People" it gave "their Ticket a kind of Mob Celebrity that is more Dangerous."[66]

Yet, whatever their private feelings, Federalists recognized the need to take expedient steps to win popular support. The organization of the Washington Benevolent Society, with its ritual, secrecy, mystery, public display, parades, costumes, and festivals represented an effort to catch "the fancy of the people" and to attract supporters from all segments of society.[67] The Federalists were even willing to change their party name in 1807 in the hope that this would help to counter popular biases. The Republican press had mockingly referred to the Federalists as "The Hog Ticket," "The Royal Ticket," and, most of all, as the "Aristocratic" party.[68] At the conclusion of the 1807 campaign, one of Foote's correspondents wrote, "If we lose the present Election . . . it will be owing to the unconquerable prejudices against the name of Federalism— & however unreasonable the thing is in itself—it must be counteracted—& the only way I see is for the leaders to follow example of their New York friends—& call themselves Americans."[69] The New York City Federalists had hoped that a new label, especially one designated "The American Ticket," would encourage "every true AMERICAN, to whatever party he may belong, to come out and give it his support."[70]

The Republicans mocked this strategy, and labeled the Federalists rogues. The change of their name was said to match the shift of their views on Morgan Lewis, from opposing him in 1804 to supporting him in 1807. To the *American Citizen,* this was "nothing short of POLITICAL PROSTITUTION . . . no thing less criminal than that of a VIRTUOUS MAN PUBLICLY TAKING TO HIS BED AND ARMS AN ABANDONED PROSTITUTE."[71] The Federalist flamboyance on election days was also derided. Their coaches, which were actively used to carry voters, "were labelled on the four sides with the largest letters— 'American ticket,' and the driver's hat was decorated with the same epithets."[72]

These elections in early nineteenth-century New York were marked by a significant increase in voter turnout. In the four gubernatorial contests prior to 1800, 68 percent of the eligible electorate had voted, but the average percentage rose to 93 for the seven elections from 1801 through 1820 (see Table 1). How can this striking 25 percent increase in voter participation be accounted for, and what does it signify?

Richard McCormick has suggested that the single key factor in explaining voter turnout is an obvious one, namely, the closeness of elections.[73] It is true, indeed, that many New York contests were close; in more than half of them the margin of victory ranged from 0.6 to 6.2 percent (see Table 2). However, the elections held after 1801, when voter participation increased sharply, were not closer than the four preceding ones. Perhaps other variables must be sought in explaining the increased voter participation in later elections. Important issues were clearly at stake in the early 1800s, but this had also been true in the 1790s.

A reasonable explanation for the higher voting turnouts is the popularization of politics, and, especially, of electioneering. It is difficult to fix a turning point in campaigning methods; many of the techniques used after 1800 were employed during the 1790s.[74] However, the data presented on campaign practices suggests that both parties made more extensive and systematic efforts to reach the entire electorate after 1800. There is little doubt, for example, that men were mobilized to vote in gubernatorial elections who did not meet the legal suffrage requirements.[75] (Surely, this is one explanation for the extraordinarily high percentage of participation by the "eligible" electorate; in some counties more than 100 percent!) Popularized electioneering efforts had the effect of fostering an informal democratization of politics.

On some occasions, the Federalists in New York did not contest assembly and senate elections, but they worked in concert every three years in efforts to win the governorship. This was a prize worth the seeking. In effect, gubernatorial politics were to New York in the first two decades of the nineteenth century what presidential politics were to national parties after the late 1820s. The triennial election was a rallying focus for coordinated and extensive campaigning efforts that went much beyond annual assembly electioneering. The Federalists found it increasingly necessary, after they lost the governorship in 1801, to employ tactics similar to the Republicans in order to get every possible voter to the polls in close elections.

The increase of voter participation in New York requires further explanation. The percentage of adult white males who voted for governor does not compare favorably with the turnout in other states (see Table 3). The reason is simply that New York had one of the most restrictive suffrage requirements in the nation for governor and state senators. However, the extent of disfranchisement for these offices has sometimes been misstated. Chilton Williamson points out that "only about 33 percent of all electors could vote for senators and governors."[76] In *Politics in New York State*, Alvin Kass reinforces this view, saying that 65 to 70 percent of adult men could vote for assembly, "although two-thirds of this group did not fulfill the more stringent demands made on those who wished to cast ballots for the governor and the senators."[77] Actually, as Table 4 demonstrates, between 50 and 62 percent of the eligible electorate *could* vote for the higher offices.

The percentage of adult white males voting for governor rose from a low of 21 percent in 1789 to a high of 41 percent in 1810. In the Northern states studied by Fischer (he includes no voting statistics for New York), the percentages went from 24 in New Hampshire in 1790 to a high of 81 in 1814; from 16 in Massachusetts in 1795 to a high of 64 in 1813 and 1814;[78] from a low of 26 in Pennsylvania in 1796 to a high of 70 in 1808; and in New Jersey legislative elections from 26 in 1796 to 70 in 1808.[79]

An interesting comparison of New York's voter participation with that of other states can be made in terms of the state's assembly or congressional results. A sampling of voter turnout for these elections shows that 74 percent of the eligible electorate participated in 18 counties in 1807, 69 percent in 43 counties in 1814, and 74 percent in 25 counties in 1820 (see Table 5).[80] (This means that more than 50 percent of the adult white males voted in these elections.) If these figures are fairly representative of percentages throughout the state, they reveal that in the most popular exercise of the suffrage (for congress and assembly), New York's voter participation was comparable to levels achieved in other Northern states.[81]

New York, alone among the Northern states, had a different and higher qualification for the gubernatorial and state senate suffrage. It would be interesting to determine whether the Federalists received a greater proportion of the vote among the more exclusive electorate, and a lower percentage among the more popular electorate. More investigation would be required for a conclusive response, but the 1816 congressional and gubernatorial campaigns show that the Democratic-Republicans received only a 2.1 percent higher portion of the vote for Congress than they did for governor.[82] In 1814 the Democratic-Republicans actually received 0.3 percent fewer votes for Congress than they got in state senate elections where the suffrage was more restricted (see Table 6). A sampling of returns in various counties from 1800 to 1816 shows that the Republicans received only a slightly higher proportion of votes in assembly and congressional elections than they earned for governor and state senators (see Table 7, and for an example of more dramatic gains in New York City, see Table 8).

The extent to which there was an absence of significant differences in the actual voting patterns of the two New York electorates may help to explain why suffrage reform did not become an important issue prior to 1820. Although some elections were very close, the need for a revamped suffrage was not imperative for the Republicans because they retained the governorship continuously after 1801. The occasional Federalist dominance of the legislature also revealed that the popular electorate could not always be counted upon to be in the Democratic-Republican column.

It is noteworthy that the great thrust for suffrage reform followed the election of 1820 in which DeWitt Clinton won the governorship, but the Clintonians lost the legislature. The political message was clear: where the suffrage was broadest, the Bucktails won; where it was limited, Clinton won. The *Albany Argus*, Van Buren's principal newspaper, summed up the situation: "Clinton is elected governor by a small majority of freehold votes over Daniel D. Tompkins, who, if the people at large had been permitted to vote, would have been placed in the chair of state, and we should have as governor a representative of the people, not of the aristocracy and of the office-holders of New York."[83]

One of Clinton's friends warned him of anticipated Bucktail responses: " 'They feel their defeat to the pith of their bones and the core of their hearts, but are recovering from their discovery and hope to revolutionize everything. . . . They talk of dividing counties—calling a State convention—extending the right of suffrage . . . and many other schemes.' "[84]

The manner in which the suffrage reform movement developed after the 1820 election may lead one to question the judgements offered by some historians on the new voting provision in the constitution of 1821. Dixon Ryan Fox regarded the change as a fulfillment of democratic principles: "The extension of the suffrage was not achieved by the eloquence of advocates; it came because it accorded with an American ideal."[85] Jabez D. Hammond wrote even more glowingly during the 1840s that this expansion of the suffrage was "unprecedented in any other part of the world. . . . In past ages, in every other country, such a change could only have been effected by physical force, here it was brought about by moral power."[86] He concludes that an "extraordinary and peaceable revolution" had been achieved by a class of men "who held the exclusive power of government in their own hands, who were invited to resign, and who voluntarily did in fact resign that power, or a portion of it, to others. Is there in history a parallel to this?"[87]

Although 30 percent of the adult white males in New York were excluded from voting in any election, and more than 40 percent of the electorate was barred from voting for the state's highest offices, there is little evidence to suggest that those who were disfranchised agitated for suffrage reform. Rather, the movement to broaden the vote in New York was primarily the consequence of the self-interest of a political party.[88] Yet, narrowly pragmatic as its objectives might have been, the Bucktail party served as an instrument for democracy by bringing about a more equitable voting law. So, too, one can note a similar impact by both parties in their electioneering practices. Although the parties themselves were often undemocratic in their structure and machinery, they tended publicly to project a democratic image. The practical objective of winning simply necessitated an increasing involvement of greater numbers of people in elections and party activities. And if the price for high voter turnouts was an assault on comity in the state because of excessive political rhetoric and the emotionalism of campaigns, the early and persistent dualism of New York parties may have helped to channel responses and to minimize the extremes of a more diverse factionalism.[89] The intensity of campaigns was still mercifully brief—usually one or two months before elections. Above all, through the early popularization of politics, both parties in the first decades of the nineteenth century gave impetus to democracy in Irving's Knickerbocker New York.

TABLE 1.
Votes for Governor, 1789–1820[1]

Year	Eligible 100 pound freeholders[1]	Total votes	Eligible electorate voting, in %
1789	19,369[2]	12,353	65[2]
1792	26,159[3]	18,000[1]	72
1795	36,338	25,373	70
1798	44,915[3]	29,644	66
1801	53,492	45,770	86
1804	62,325[3]	52,968	85
1807	71,159	66,063	93
1810	78,159[3]	79,578	102
1813	85,158[3]	83,042	98
1816	91,824[3]	84,059	92
1820	98,633	93,437	96

1. A freeholder, according to practice derived from English common law, was a person holding property for at least his own lifetime. For the freeholder to be eligible to vote for governor, the freehold had to have a tax evaluation of at least 100 pounds. Data on qualified freeholders and gubernatorial votes from: New York (State), Secretary of State, *Census of the State of New York for 1855* (Albany: 1857); p. x; Alfred F. Young, *The Democratic Republicans of New York* (Chapel Hill: The University of North Carolina Press, 1967), pp. 587–89; Richard P. McCormick, "Suffrage Classes and Party Alignments: A Study in Voter Behavior," *Mississippi Valley Historical Review* (December 1959), p. 405.
2. The number of freeholders is based on the 1790 census; therefore, the percentages of voter participation are on the low side.
3. When data for 100 pound freeholders was unavailable, figures were calculated on the basis of an even rate of increase between those years in which census data was taken (1790, 1795, 1801, 1807, 1814, 1821). The figures thus extrapolated apparently underestimate the number of eligible voters.
4. Includes disputed votes; see Young, *op. cit.*, p. 589.

TABLE 2.
Margin of Victory in Gubernatorial Elections, 1789–1820

Year	Federalist	Total vote, in %	Democratic-Republicans	Total vote, in %	Margin of victory, in %
1789[1]	5,962	48.3	6,391	51.7	3.4
1792[1]	8,332	49.7	8,440	50.3	0.6
1795[1]	13,481	53.1	11,892	46.9	6.2
1798[2]	16,012	54.0	13,632	46.0	8.0
1801[3]	20,962	45.8	24,808	54.2	8.4
1804[3]	22,139	41.8	30,829	58.2	16.4
1807[4]	30,989	46.9	35,074	53.1	6.2
1810[5]	36,484	45.8	43,094	54.2	8.4
1813[6]	39,718	47.9	43,324	52.1	4.2
1816[7]	38,647	45.8	45,412	54.2	8.4
1820[8]	47,447	50.8	45,990	49.2	1.6

1. Young, *Democratic-Republicans, op. cit.*, pp. 587–89.
2. DeAlva S. Alexander, *A Political History of the State of New York* (New York: 1906), I, 82.
3. *New York American Citizen*, June 13, 1804.
4. *Ibid.*, June 12, 1807.
5. Alexander, *op. cit.*, I, 179.
6. *Albany Register*, June 8, 1813.
7. *Albany Argus*, May 31, 1816.
8. John Anthony Casais, "The New York Constitutional Convention of 1821 and Its Aftermath" (Columbia University, Unpublished Doctoral Dissertation, 1967), p. 202.

TABLE 3.

Percentage of Voter Participation in Elections in Five States, 1789–1826[1]

Year	New York	New Hampshire	Massachusetts	New Jersey[2]	Pennsylvania
1789	21				
1790		24	17	27	31
1792	23	27	17		
1793		29	18		27
1795	30	27	16		
1796		30	24	26	26
1798	28	33	18	46	
1801	37	40	37		
1804	37	60	41		
1805		68	47		55
1807	39	39	58		
1808		36	56	70	70
1810	41	71	61		
1813	38	75	64		
1814		81	64	67	43
1816	36	77	59		
1817		70	50		61
1820	32	45	47		64
1824	58	54	58	31	
1826	54	52	30	40	28

1. Percentages are in terms of adult white males or free adult males. With the exception of the New York data, statistics are taken from David Hackett Fischer, *The Revolution of American Conservatism* (New York: Harper & Row, 1965), p. 188.
2. All elections gubernatorial except New Jersey, which was legislative.

TABLE 4.

Percentage of Electorate Eligible to Vote for Governor and Senators, 1790–1821

Year	Adult white males (est.)[1]	Total voters	100 pound freeholders	100 pound freeholders as % of AWM	% of electorate eligible for Governor and Senators
1790[2]	66,839	38,824	19,369	29	50
1795[2]	92,455	64,017	36,338	39	57
1801[3]	125,000	86,767	53,492	43	62
1807[4]	170,000	121,289	71,159	42	59
1814[4]	239,000	151,826	87,491	37	58
1821[4]	299,500	202,510	100,490	34	50

1. Adult white men estimates based on U.S. Census Bureau Reports. Estimates assume even population growth on a yearly basis.
2. Young, *Democratic-Republicans, op. cit.*, pp. 587–88.
3. New York *American Citizen and General Advertiser*, March 24, 1802.
4. Voting figures from New York (State), Secretary of State, *Census of State of New York for 1855* (Albany: 1857), p. x.

TABLE 5.

Percentage of Eligible Electorate Actually Voting in Assembly (1807) and Congressional (1814) Elections

1807

County	Total electors[1]	Actual assembly voters[2]	Eligible electorate actually voting, in %
Clinton	1,358	647	48
Columbia	4,525	4,100	91
Dutchess	6,752	4,719	73
Herkimer	2,974	2,308	78
Jefferson	1,988	1,262	63
Kings	997	800	80
Lewis	1,096	742	68
New York	12,354	9,357	76
Oneida	5,408	4,273	79
Onondaga	3,692	2,650	71
Orange	3,714	2,963	80
Queens	2,707	1,750	65
Richmond	711	656	92
St. Lawrence	860	328	38
Saratoga	4,426	3,098	70
Seneca	1,604	1,039	71
Ulster	3,851	2,820	73
Washington	5,038	3,980	79

1. New York (State), *Census of New York for 1855*, (Albany: 1857), p. x.
2. Voting results from May and June issues of *New-York American Citizen* and *New-York Herald*.

1814

County	Total electors[1]	Actual vote for Congress[2]	Eligible electorate actually voting, in %
Albany	5,476	2,780	50
Allegany	619	253	49
Broome	1,529	963	63
Cayuga	5,526	3,485	63
Chautauqua	640	552	86
Chenango	3,752	2,458	66
Clinton	1,293	947	73
Columbia	5,317	3,886	73
Cortland	1,540	1,080	64
Delaware	3,127	2,087	67
Dutchess	6,684	4,085	61
Essex	1,766	1,250	71
Franklin	452	357	79
Genesee	3,985	2,676	67
Greene	2,861	2,096	73
Herkimer	3,438	2,514	73
Jefferson	2,787	2,265	81
Kings	1,225	969	79
Lewis	1,184	745	63
Madison	4,012	2,778	69
Montgomery	6,437	4,860	75
New York	13,921	10,399	75
Niagara	1,451	882	61

(Table continued on next page)

TABLE 5. (Continued)

1814

County	Total electors[1]	Actual vote for Congress[2]	Eligible electorate actually voting, in %
Oneida	6,916	4,980	72
Onondaga	4,678	3,016	64
Ontario	9,096	6,495	71
Orange	5,020	3,005	60
Otsego	6,402	5,209	81
Putnam	1,499	925	62
Queens	3,210	2,086	62
Rensselaer	5,924	4,423	75
St. Lawrence	1,456	998	69
Saratoga	5,120	3,739	73
Schenectady	1,845	1,415	77
Schoharie	3,244	2,350	72
Seneca	3,270	1,845	56
Steuben	1,831	871	48
Suffolk	3,709	2,375	64
Sullivan	1,047	776	74
Tioga	1,589	704	44
Ulster	4,189	2,675	64
Warren	1,321	1,064	81
Washington	5,487	4,507	82

1. New York (State), *Census of New York for 1855* (Albany: 1857), p. x.
2. *Albany Argus,* June 7, 1814.

TABLE 6.

Distribution of County Votes by Party Affiliation, 1814[1]

County	Congress Democratic-Republicans Votes	%	Federalists Votes	%	State Senate Democratic-Republicans Votes	%	Federalists Votes	%	Democratic-Republicans change in Congress over Senate, in %
Suffolk	1,857	78.2	518	21.8	1,623	78.4	445	21.6	– 0.2
New York	5,272	50.7	5,127	49.3	1,646	50.4	1,800	49.6	0.3
Kings	490	50.6	479	49.4	310	48.7	326	51.3	1.9
Queens	862	41.3	1,224	58.7	619	42.0	855	58.0	– 0.7
Dutchess	1,888	46.2	2,197	53.8	1,205	44.2	1,520	55.8	2.0
Putnam	659	71.2	266	28.8	447	73.2	162	26.8	– 2.0
Columbia	1,475	37.9	2,411	62.1	1,164	41.9	1,611	58.1	– 4.0
Orange	2,345	78.0	660	22.0	1,761	76.5	541	23.5	1.5
Ulster	1,483	55.4	1,192	44.6	1,109	56.4	857	43.6	– 1.0
Sullivan	469	60.4	307	39.6	339	63.0	199	37.0	– 2.6
Delaware	1,263	60.5	824	39.5	951	64.6	521	35.4	– 4.1
Greene	951	45.4	1,144	54.6	671	44.3	845	55.7	– 1.1
Albany	1,003	36.1	1,777	63.9	900	38.7	1,424	61.3	– 2.6
Rensselaer	1,860	42.1	2,563	57.9	1,256	41.7	1,752	58.3	– 0.4
Saratoga	2,183	58.4	1,556	41.6	1,649	60.0	1,089	40.0	– 1.6
Clinton	481	50.8	466	49.2	285	53.6	247	46.4	– 2.8
Franklin	87	24.4	270	75.6	39	20.9	148	79.1	3.5
Warren	652	61.3	412	38.7	424	65.2	226	34.8	– 3.9
Washington	2,235	49.6	2,272	50.4	1,551	50.4	1,528	49.6	– 0.8
Essex	715	57.2	535	42.8	388	58.2	275	41.8	– 1.0
Schenectady	782	55.3	633	44.7	538	56.2	419	43.8	– 0.9
Schoharie	1,362	58.0	928	42.0	976	60.3	643	39.7	– 2.3
Montgomery	2,340	48.1	2,520	51.9	1,779	50.4	1,749	49.6	– 2.3
Chenango	1,631	66.4	827	33.6	1,167	64.5	641	35.5	1.9
Otsego	2,751	52.8	2,458	47.2	1,742	51.5	1,641	48.5	1.3
Broome	447	46.4	516	53.6	331	47.7	363	52.3	– 1.3
Oneida	2,159	43.4	2,821	56.6	1,691	42.5	2,291	57.5	0.9
Madison	1,374	49.5	1,404	50.5	961	47.2	1,075	52.8	2.3
Herkimer	1,408	56.0	1,106	44.0	982	57.1	738	42.9	– 1.1
Jefferson	1,082	47.8	1,183	52.2	829	50.1	825	49.9	– 2.3
Lewis	435	58.4	310	41.6	295	56.0	232	44.0	2.4
St. Lawrence	345	34.6	653	65.4	323	37.8	531	62.2	– 3.2
Onondaga	1,790	59.3	1,226	40.7	1,301	58.1	937	41.9	1.2
Cortland	624	57.8	456	42.2	566	57.8	413	42.2	0.0
Cayuga	2,485	71.3	1,000	28.7	1,789	71.5	714	28.5	– 0.2
Seneca	1,354	73.4	491	26.6	893	70.6	371	29.4	2.8
Tioga	630	89.5	74	10.5	325	74.2	105	25.8	15.3
Steuben	599	68.8	272	31.2	235	55.6	188	44.4	13.2
Ontario	3,243	49.9	3,252	50.1	1,997	48.6	2,108	51.4	1.3
Allegany	168	66.4	85	33.6	184	57.0	139	43.0	9.4
Genesee	1,709	63.9	967	36.1	1,249	67.0	616	33.0	– 3.1
Niagara	574	65.1	308	34.9	385	63.0	226	37.0	2.1
Chautauqua	252	45.7	300	54.3	234	45.7	278	54.3	0.0

1. Voting data from *Albany Argus*, June 7, 1814.

TABLE 7.

Distribution of County Votes by Party Affiliation, 1800–1815[1]

Year	County	Senate or Governor Federalist votes	Democratic-Republicans Votes	%	Congress or Assembly Federalist votes	Democratic-Republicans Votes	%	Democratic-Republicans change in lower houses, in %
1800	Kings	138	255	64.9	238	338	58.7	− 6.2
1800	Richmond	302	23	07.1	316	41	11.5	4.4
1800	Queens	450	570	55.9	762	830	52.1	− 3.8
1800	New York	1,125	875	43.7	2,640	3,080	53.8	10.1
1800	Orange	270	1,230	82.0	395	1,760	81.2	− 0.8
1800	Suffolk	303	865	74.1	458	1,059	69.8	− 4.3
1801	New York	1,092	1,226	52.9	2,168	3,651	62.7	9.8
1802	Columbia	1,008	1,018	50.2	1,620	1,525	48.5	− 1.7
1802	Greene	373	346	48.1	528	531	50.1	2.0
1802	Delaware	240	487	67.0	343	636	65.0	− 2.0
1803	Oneida	1,404	1,205	46.2	1,687	1,361	44.6	− 1.6
1803	Delaware	327	590	64.3	476	746	61.0	− 3.3
1803	Ulster	469	776	62.3	940	1,130	54.6	− 7.7
1803	Montgomery	735	1,400	65.6	981	1,750	64.1	− 1.5
1803	Dutchess	916	1,351	59.6	1,479	2,020	57.7	− 1.9
1803	New York	1,198	1,124	48.4	2,764	3,452	55.5	7.1
1803	Richmond	208	180	46.4	218	304	58.2	11.8
1803	Greene	432	420	49.3	540	540	50.0	0.7
1804	Washington	1,029	1,678	62.0	1,000	2,367	70.3	8.3
1804	Columbia	1,291	1,162	47.4	1,926	1,606	48.3	0.9
1804	Albany	1,591	1,189	42.8	1,440	1,893	56.8	14.0
1804	Rensselaer	1,123	1,388	55.3	1,490	1,880	55.8	0.5
1804	Oneida	1,782	2,165	54.9	2,131	2,227	51.1	− 3.8
1804	Kings	218	244	52.8	287	323	53.0	0.2
1804	Dutchess	1,461	1,409	49.1	1,658	2,289	58.0	8.9
1804	Ulster	680	1,138	62.6	787	1,492	65.4	1.8
1804	Greene	620	644	50.9	791	863	52.2	1.3
1806	Westchester	618	674	52.2	952	898	48.5	− 3.7
1807	Columbia	1,507	1,299	46.3	2,246	1,889	45.7	− 0.6
1807	Dutchess	2,035	1,073	34.5	3,133	1,586	33.6	− 0.9
1807	Oneida	1,830	1,779	49.3	2,200	2,075	48.5	− 0.8
1807	Kings	177	250	58.5	289	377	56.6	− 1.9
1807	Herkimer	610	1,105	64.4	800	1,470	64.8	0.4
1807	New York	1,787	1,600	47.2	4,450	4,860	52.2	5.0
1807	Saratoga	935	1,725	64.8	1,040	2,050	66.3	1.5
1808	New York	1,581	1,572	49.9	4,521	5,635	55.5	5.6
1808	Queens	640	590	48.0	950	790	45.4	− 2.6
1808	Greene	857	515	36.7	1,176	781	39.8	3.2
1808	Kings	254	280	52.4	422	397	48.4	− 4.0
1808	Madison	1,040	1,035	49.9	1,250	1,160	48.1	− 1.8
1808	Jefferson	515	670	56.5	600	770	56.2	− 0.3
1808	Otsego	1,160	1,350	53.8	1,510	1,720	53.3	− 0.5
1808	Oneida	2,000	1,620	44.7	2,500	2,000	44.4	− 0.3
1809	Queens	823	671	44.9	1,188	967	44.9	0.0
1809	New York	1,530	1,361	47.1	4,900	5,026	50.6	3.6
1809	Westchester	1,048	950	57.5	1,411	1,326	48.4	0.9
1809	Seneca	335	524	61.1	504	887	63.8	2.7
1809	Herkimer	818	846	50.8	1,362	1,348	49.9	− 0.8
1809	Montgomery	1,828	1,569	46.2	2,602	2,192	43.6	− 2.6
1809	Madison	1,279	866	40.4	1,584	1,148	42.0	1.6
1809	Broome	396	345	46.6	554	450	44.8	− 1.8

(Table continued on next page)

TABLE 7. (Continued)

Year	County	Senate or Governor Federalist votes	Democratic-Republicans Votes	%	Congress or Assembly Federalist votes	Democratic-Republicans Votes	%	Democratic-Republicans change in lower houses, in %
1809	Saratoga	1,153	1,557	57.5	1,485	2,003	57.4	− 0.1
1810	New York	2,000	1,726	46.1	5,322	5,278	49.8	3.7
1810	Queens	780	801	50.7	1,121	1,081	49.5	− 1.2
1810	Columbia	2,134	1,608	45.6	2,598	2,012	43.6	− 2.0
1810	Cayuga	580	1,891	76.5	694	2,155	75.6	− 0.9
1811	Columbia	1,507	1,238	45.1	2,187	1,822	45.4	0.3
1811	Queens	781	583	42.8	1,141	833	42.2	− 0.6
1811	Kings	325	320	49.6	537	542	50.2	0.6
1812	Queens	793	548	40.9	1,121	908	44.7	3.8
1812	Columbia	1,597	1,187	42.6	2,346	1,813	43.6	1.0
1813	Washington	1,934	1,970	50.5	2,784	2,816	50.3	− 0.2
1813	Columbia	1,780	1,264	41.5	2,547	1,691	40.0	− 1.5
1815	Cayuga	643	1,905	74.4	780	2,445	75.8	1.4

1. For this sampling of election returns, the Democratic-Republicans received 50.9 percent of votes cast for the higher offices, and 52.9 percent of votes for assembly and congress. Their improvement in the elections with an expanded suffrage was only 2.0 percent.

TABLE 8.

Distribution of Votes by Party Affiliation in

New York City, 1800–1816

Year	Senate or Governor Federalist votes	Democratic-Republicans Votes	%	Congress or Assembly Federalist votes	Democratic-Republicans Votes	%	Democratic-Republicans gain in lower houses, in %[1]
1800	1,125	875	43.7	2,640	3,080	53.8	10.1
1801	1,090	1,266	53.7	2,168	3,651	62.8	9.1
1803	1,198	1,124	48.4	2,764	3,452	55.5	7.1
1804	1,415	1,315	48.2	2,700	3,495	56.4	8.2
1807	1,787	1,600	47.2	4,450	4,860	52.2	5.0
1808	1,581	1,572	49.9	4,521	5,635	55.5	5.6
1809	1,530	1,361	47.1	4,900	5,026	50.6	3.5
1810	1,994	1,666	45.5	5,322	5,278	49.8	4.3
1811	1,937	1,264	39.5	5,267	3,901	42.6	3.1
1812	1,884	1,380	42.3	4,816	4,345	47.4	5.1
1813	1,999	1,626	44.9	5,050	4,903	49.3	4.4
1814	1,900	1,646	46.4	5,210	5,349	50.7	4.3
1815	1,888	1,351	41.7	4,747	4,690	49.7	8.0
1816	1,926	1,861	49.2	4,809	5,912	55.1	5.9

1. In this period, the average Democratic gain in the lower houses was 5.6 percent.

New York Society: High and Low

James F. Richardson

Like generals who employ the tactics and strategy of the previous war, growing nineteenth-century cities faced new and complex problems with ideas and institutions developed in simpler, less demanding times. Nowhere was this more apparent than in Washington Irving's native city. During his youth, the liberation of the creative energies of the free individual seemed to be the path to social well-being. Each man diligently pursuing his self-interest would raise the overall wealth of society and provide for a distribution of resources on the basis of social worth. Those who made the greatest contribution to growth and prosperity deserved the greatest rewards; those who were poor had demonstrated their unworthiness.[1] Government had a few simple tasks which did not require continuity of officeholding or a formal bureaucracy. Social problems could be handled by voluntary individual or small-group action and an elite could presume to act in the interests of all citizens.[2]

The growth that resulted from New York City's emergence as the key node of a burgeoning national economy made many of these ideas and the institutions embodying them obsolete. In 1809, when Irving's *A History of New York* was published, New York had fewer than 100,000 people; by the time of Irving's death 50 years later, there were more than 800,000 people living on Manhattan Island, with an additional 200,000 in nearby suburbs. New York had ship and telegraph connections with most of the rest of the United States, and for a short time in the late 1850s the Atlantic Cable cut to a fraction the time required for sending messages to Europe. The cable soon failed and did not go into permanent operation until after the Civil War.[3]

Despite the problems involved in developing the cable, New York's external communications and relations were more fully developed than its internal structure. Midcentury Gotham had grown beyond the capacity of its own institutions to service, govern, or even understand the city. Ambitious men in search of wealth and social position had succeeded in forging links between Alabama cotton fields, New York shipping and finance, and Liverpool markets; but no one brought the Five Points, the city's most notorious slum area, and Washington Square together. Rich and poor scarcely inhabited the same moral universe. The city's government was overwhelmed by the multiplicity and complexity of its tasks. Three quarters of a million people in constricted space posed burdens that a government designed in a smaller, less complex city could not meet. Sewers overflowed, privies fouled wells, streets went uncleaned; and the poor, crowded in tenements, cellars, and shanties sickened and died with fearsome rapidity.[4]

The problem of order seemed almost insurmountable. Residents and visitors alike viewed the city's streets as unpredictable and sometimes unsafe and physically dangerous. Comfortable and prosperous people, even when they manifested sympathy for the plight of the poor, expressed more concern about the establishment of social control. They founded bible and tract associations, benevolent societies, schools, and a police force in hopes of creating social order and discipline.[5] And, in fact, they had reason to be concerned. The New York State census of 1855 showed that more than half of the city's population had been born outside the United States. The largest single group was the Irish, who constituted more than a quarter of the total population. Many of the Irish had fled from the effects of famine and destitution in their homeland with few, if any, resources. They lacked money, skills, and the experience of living in a complex urban community. Many of the Irish were not farmers in the old country, with all of the varied skills that successful farming demands, but rather rural laborers who lived by planting and digging potatoes.[6]

Truly uprooted, they faced the task of survival in an alien, hostile environment, which had a surplus of unskilled labor and which scorned their religion and derided their culture. The social and personal costs were high as many of them succumbed to alcoholism, insanity, pauperism, and crime. The ratio of individuals of a given nativity convicted in New York's courts of special sessions in 1859 compared to the total number of that group counted in the census of 1860 shows an extraordinarily high rate for the Irish, 5.5 percent, in contrast to 1.2 percent for Germans and 0.9 percent for native Americans. Drunk and disorderly was the most common charge leveled against the Irish, accounting for more than one-half of all their convictions. This statistic indicated the extent of alcohol abuse among them, and the authorities' willingness to use punitive legal mechanisms in such cases. Similarly, the American-born children of Irish parents were committed to the House of Refuge for juvenile delinquents at a far higher rate than the children of Germans and native Americans. Comparable figures could be quoted for other measures of inability to move through life without running afoul of the law or requiring institutional care.[7]

Most of the Irish occupied a precarious place in the urban economy. Their lack of skills and the prevailing prejudice against them meant severe disadvantages in the labor market. More than half of all the gainfully employed Irish in 1855 were in three occupational categories: domestic servants, laborers, and dressmakers and seamstresses. In many instances the category of "laborer" meant a dependence upon the casual labor market where supply usually outran demand. Men so positioned had great difficulty providing any kind of decent food and shelter for themselves and their families or finding a place in society and accepting its disciplines. Women had either to hope for a place as domestic servants or try to earn a living as seamstresses.[8] Contemporaries such as George Foster, whose *New York in Slices* appeared in 1849, and E. H. Chapin, a religious writer of the 1850s, stressed the plight of the city's sewing women, forced to endless toil to maintain subsistence.[9]

The commercial and industrial giant that was New York in the 1850s demanded a strong sense of individual discipline and

THE GREAT FIRE of the CITY of NEW-YORK, 16 DECEMBER 1835.

Published January 1836 by the Proprietor, H. R. Robinson, No 48 Courtland Street, New York

A contemporary depiction of what Washington Irving wrote of
in a family letter of Dec. 25, 1835, as "our late calamitous fire."
The response of municipal authorities, and private citizens, as
shown, exemplifies the courageous Knickerbocker spirit,
even in adversity. From I. N. Phelps Stokes, *The Iconography
of Manhattan Island* (New York, 1918).

responsibility from its residents. The city could function best only if each person accepted the constraints imposed by congestion and a multiplicity of casual, unplanned human contacts.[10] That many citizens did not or could not accept such responsibility was all too apparent. Poorer immigrants deviated most widely, but others also had problems in adjusting to a city that was not simply an enlarged version of the preindustrial community but a new kind of entity. A sense of civility, a recognition of common bonds and common human needs proved hard to come by in a city wracked by class, ethnic, and racial tensions, which lacked instruments to deal with these tensions through processes of accommodation.[11]

New York, like other American cities, allocated scarce resources on the basis of the marketplace with its key question of what do you want, what are you willing and able to pay. The market provided the only instrument of communication among all of the diverse elements of the city. New York could not achieve the collective discipline of allocating such key items as income and space by any other mechanism. Those with the greatest resources flourished in the marketplace, while others, the majority, found their essential human needs in housing and security of income unmet.[12]

The city grew so rapidly that the poor could not be housed in the hand-me-down housing of the better-off. Many of both rich and poor had to live in new construction, and rapidly growing cities in many countries and cultures show some horrendous results. In New York of the 1850s new construction for the poor consisted of tenements in the built-up portions of the city and squatters' shanties on the outskirts. Tenements, buildings specifically designed and built as slums, spread over most of the lower portions of Manhattan. When Central Park was built in the 1850s, considerably north of the developed areas, the police had to evict squatters and pull down their shanties to allow construction of Olmsted and Vaux's "Greensward." In 1864, a census taken by sanitary inspectors and police showed more than a half million people living in tenements and cellars, with an additional uncounted number surviving in shanties. The tenements, profitable to their owners and managers, provided little or nothing in the way of air, light, water, or means of escape from fire for the bulk of their residents. Agitation for some form of regulation began in the 1850s, but not until 1901 was a meaningful tenement house law passed. The shanties remind one of the dwellings characteristic of Latin America's *favelas* where the poor who cannot afford urban housing throw up some form of shelter on the periphery of the city, with no water or sanitary facilities available. The results in New York of the 1850s and contemporary Indian or Latin American cities are similar: widespread sickness and death.[13]

New York's death rate in the 1850s approached 35 per thousand, a ratio higher than that of 1810. Disease and premature death did not, like the rain, fall upon rich and poor alike. Slum sections of the city had much higher morbidity and mortality rates than more affluent areas, leading some moralists to conclude that God punished paupers for their vicious, ignorant, and dissolute ways. This moralistic contempt of the poor often coincided with a religious determination to improve the spiritual and material condition of the downtrodden through environmental reform. Men such as Louis Pease of the Five Points House of Industry and Robert Hartley of the Association for Improving the Condition of the Poor came to look upon the slum as both cause and effect of alcoholism and dependency. After the draft riots of 1863, sanitary reformers led by Dr. Stephen Smith built upon the observations made by visitors for religious missions and charitable institutions to document systematically the housing and environmental conditions of the poor. A London physician, Dr. John Snow, in the previous decade had demonstrated the relationship between fouled water and the spread of cholera.

In the face of a threatened cholera epidemic in New York City, sanitary and medical reformers succeeded in overcoming inertia, religious resistance to the authority of science, and the hostility of property owners and the poor to official interference to establish the Metropolitan Board of Health in 1866. This board, which worked closely with the police, had broad powers

to order tenement owners to clean their buildings and residents
to part with their pigs. New York City suffered far less from cholera in 1866 than it had in previous epidemics in 1832 and 1849.
Medical science now knew something about the etiology of the
disease, and comfortable people accepted environmentalist as
well as moralistic explanations of poverty and disease.[14]

The most obvious way for middle- and upper-class people to
escape environmental problems was to move away to less
crowded and more pleasant surroundings. During Washington
Irving's lifetime, prosperous people wished to separate themselves as much as possible from the poor, but they could do so
only to a limited degree. Until the late 1820s, New York, like all
other urban areas, was a walking city. Workers, whether laborers, clerks, or merchants, wanted to be as close as possible to
the docks, the focal point of economic activity of the essentially
commercial city. Those able to pay the highest prices for housing lived closest to their businesses or jobs. In the late 1820s, the
omnibus, a clumsy vehicle capable of carrying 12 to 20 passen-
gers, made possible some greater separation of work and residence for the more affluent segment of the population. Merchants and attorneys could now travel from above Fourteenth
Street to their counting houses and offices. Commuter railroads
served some of the most affluent from the 1830s on. However, it
was not until the 1850s that the introduction and spread of the
horse-drawn street railway provided improved land transportation for a significant number of people. Horses could pull heav-
ier loads faster on rails laid on the streets than they could on the
surfaces of those streets. The cost of this travel restricted its
use to better-paid workers. (Even with a five cent fare, workers
who earned a dollar or a dollar and a half a day—when they
could get work—probably walked more often than they rode.)
In the late 1840s, improved ferry service opened Brooklyn and
New Jersey communities to New York commuters.[15]

Steam ferries and street railways expanded the physical area
of the city. The horse cars made an average speed of four to six
miles an hour. If we assume that a half-hour traveling time represented the acceptable maxim, those who could afford the fare

could now live two to three miles from their work. Taking City Hall as a central point, this put the possible commuting range to about Forty-second Street. The maps in the Regional Plan's Survey of the history of land use show that the fully built-up portions of the city in 1858 extended only to that point on the East Side and slightly north of it on the West Side. However, the state census of 1855 showed that more than half (57 percent) of the city's total population remained south of Fourteenth Street, or on about one-tenth of Manhattan's land area.[16]

The congestion of the lower parts of the city was even greater than these figures indicate because of the increasing amounts of land taken for commercial and industrial purposes. Much of the area south of Canal Street lost population in the 1850s as warehouses, factories, and stores encroached upon formerly residential areas. People displaced in the lower wards increased the population of the densely packed slum areas between Canal and Fourteenth Streets. Most buildings in the 1850s were only three or four stories in height; rarely did they go to six stories. More than 350,000 people, therefore, lived in low-rise buildings on less than three square miles of land which they had to share with most of the economic activities of the nation's leading commercial and industrial center.[17]

In his stimulating study *Boss Tweed's New York*, Seymour Mandelbaum suggested that physical separation between classes and groups in a city of limited internal communications inhibited mutual understanding and the development of a sense of community.[18] Certainly the more fortunate separated themselves as much as possible from the less fortunate as did natives from immigrants. The point is that most could not move very far; like it or not, a variety of social classes and ethnic groups had to live fairly close to each other. George Templeton Strong, lawyer and diarist, commuted to his downtown office from Twenty-first Street. In doing so he had to share space both on the streets and in the cars with people for whom he had no use. The ragged children of the poor infested Broadway, the city's leading commercial row. Poverty was not invisible in the 1850s, and while the sight of young girls made prematurely aged and depraved by poverty moved Strong, his more usual response was disgust and a sense of defilement.[19] Nor was the tenement confined south of Fourteenth Street. Tenement districts developed within a block or two of fashionable residential enclaves, and few people could isolate themselves completely from the disturbing sights, sounds, and smells of poverty, strange dialects and languages, and cultural patterns almost incomprehensible to native American Protestants.

Distance is a relative concept, and despite the clustering of people of similar backgrounds, most New Yorkers of the 1850s still had to share some of their social space with men, women, and children who were different. Thus, in 1855, no ward in the city had fewer than one-third of its population foreign-born; and all but one had more than 40 percent foreign-born. Those wards classified as Irish or German in every instance had fewer than half their population born in the particular country. Much of the native-born population may have been children of the dominant immigrant group; still there were often substantial numbers of other nationalities present. The Irish in particular lived throughout the city. In only four of 22 wards did the Irish constitute fewer than 20 percent of the total population; three of these four wards had heavy German concentrations. The chances were that New Yorkers, no matter where they lived, came in frequent contact with first- and second-generation Irish-Americans.[20]

In the first decades of mass immigration proximity could and did lead to hostility as often or more often than it did to communication.[21] Among the working classes, points of conflict involved housing and jobs as well as cultural style. Robert Ernst documented the "virulent economic nativism" of the 1840s as native mechanics and skilled workers tried to maintain their positions against lower-wage immigrant competition. Recent arrivals, desperate for work and unaware of American wage scales, accepted terms below those common in a trade. The flood of new arrivals speeded up the disintegration of the apprenticeship system, already in decay because of new methods of production and new systems of organization. In the early 1850s, native- and foreign-born, anxious to strengthen their bargaining power and recognizing the costs of being divided and therefore conquerable, cooperated in many unions. The cyclical downturn of 1854–55 and the effects of the Panic of 1857 weakened or destroyed many of these unions.[22]

The native Americans least able to resist immigrant economic penetration or achieve cooperation were the blacks. The city's Negro population declined in the pre-Civil War decades as foreign, especially Irish, workers replaced blacks as porters, stevedores, domestic servants, and waiters. Blacks might still be employed as strikebreakers, which further inflamed racial hatreds. Negroes constituted less than 2 percent of the city's total population, compared to the one-quarter born in Ireland; still the hostility between these groups, especially Irish aggression against blacks, contributed substantially to the city's violence and disorder in the 1850s and 1860s. The climax came in the draft riots of 1863 in which predominantly Irish mobs killed 11 blacks, often by lynching and mutilation. An unknown number of rioters and bystanders, perhaps reaching into the hundreds, died as a result of police and military suppression of the disorders. Many Irish workers believed that emancipation and the use of Negro troops would mean a horde of freedmen migrating from the South to take their jobs and violate their women. The tensions which culminated in July 1863 had their roots in the economic competition and racist hatreds of the 1840s and 1850s.[23]

Within the white population, differences of religious belief and cultural style caused social cleavages as severe as those resulting from economic competition. Antipopery had a long history in Protestant America, and the appearance of a papal legate in the 1850s created riots in a number of cities. Prohibitionist sentiment grew as native Americans sought to distinguish their behavior from that of immigrant users of alcohol and to impose this conception of morality upon newcomers. New York State adopted a prohibition law in 1855. The Court of Appeals declared the act, which had never been enforced in New York City, unconstitutional the following year. Increasingly the city divided politically on religious grounds as the Irish swelled the

ranks of Tammany and their opponents moved into the Know-
Nothing and later Republican movements. Many Tammanyites
had a strong streak of nativism, but Tammany's leaders had decided in the 1840s that cultivating Catholic immigrants made
sense. The census of 1855 indicated the wisdom of that decision
when it reported almost as many naturalized as native voters. In
nine wards naturalized voters outnumbered native-born voters.
In addition, the city contained more than 230,000 aliens, many
of whom might later join the ranks of Tammany.[24]

In cultural matters generally, Irish and Germans struggled to
maintain their identity. The Irish resisted attempts on the part of
Protestant missions and charitable institutions to uplift them,
and official Catholic hostility to Protestant-oriented public school-
ing is well-known. However, schools, whether public or pa-
rochial, reached only a fraction of the city's children in the
1850s; streets, much more than schools, were the key areas of
socialization. The Germans clung to their language and their traditions of the continental Sunday, a convivial day of music and
beer-drinking and the antithesis of the Puritan Sabbath. Native
Americans often looked on these practices as immoral and won-
dered how they could maintain the purity of their institutions in
the face of large-scale immigration.[25]

Irish addiction to whiskey and the commitment of some Germans to socialism as well as beer led natives to consider them
"the dangerous classes." Much of the city's political history of
the 1850s revolved around attempts of native Americans in the
city and state governments to restrict the power of the immi-
grant-backed Democrats. In 1857 the Republican legislature imposed a new charter and police system upon the predominantly
Democratic city. These arrangements were designed to reduce
majority rule and guarantee a strong minority voice in police
and political matters generally. Prosperous Americans welcomed
immigrants for their labor but feared their participation in politics and their impact upon American cultural homogeneity.[26]

Thus, while most New Yorkers had to share some of their social space with others, they resisted the integration of newcomers into the city's political and cultural life. George Templeton

Strong in 1857 expressed a belief that, "Our Celtic fellow citizens are almost as remote from us in temperament and constitution as the Chinese."[27] Only as the Irish gained substantially in numbers of voters and respectability, which to a considerable extent meant adopting the cultural patterns of native Americans, would they be accepted. This did not begin to happen until the 1870s when a John Kelly could live in Murray Hill, marry a niece of the first American cardinal, and make claims for political and social acceptance.[28] Obviously not all the Irish so qualified, and "reformers" would challenge the legitimacy of Irish leadership from the time of Kelly to that of Charles F. Murphy and beyond. Tammany's leaders usually remained in power because their political style seemed more in keeping with the beliefs and aspirations of the majority of the city's voters—of immigrant origin and working- and lower-middle-class status—than did the political style of the patricians.[29]

For the pre-Civil War years, the paramount issue for most immigrants was survival. Their children and grandchildren might worry about recognition, wealth, and power; the foreign-born themselves often had their hands full getting along from day to day. They labored, drank, and fought in a competitive, disorderly city, which rewarded a few and wore out many. Slum life had its gratifications, such as seeing a local boy make good in politics or on the stage, and whooping it up on Saturday night; yet the appalling death rates remind us that for many of the poor life could not be sustained in the harsh conditions of mid-nineteenth-century New York. We must also remember that as bad as life in New York was, it was usually substantially better than in those places from which the poor had come.

For the upper levels of New York society life could be very pleasant. The poor might be disturbingly visible; Broadway in winter could be, as George Templeton Strong described it, "a long canal of mud syrup, all the sidewalks greasy with an abominable compound like melted black butter"; and the city's government might be in the hands of demagogues and scoundrels; still, the good things in life predominated.[31]

In a recent examination of "The Egalitarian Myth and the

American Social Reality: Wealth, Mobility, and Equality in the 'Era of the Common Man,' " Edward Pessen concluded that the rich were overwhelmingly of privileged origins and that they grew wealthier during the Jacksonian period. He estimates that in 1845 the richest 1 percent of New York's population owned one-half of the city's wealth, while the upper 4 percent owned more than four-fifths of the city's total wealth. Furthermore, three-fourths of the wealthiest families of the 1850s had occupied a similar position a generation earlier. Continuity of wealth over the generations was the rule rather than the exception. Only 2 to 6 percent of the nation's urban rich came from poor or middling origins. The wealthier an individual's family the greater the chances of augmenting his wealth substantially. The myth of rags to riches was just that, a myth, useful in holding allegiance to the economic order and encouraging diligence and aggressiveness among the young in hopes that they might reap great rewards, but inaccurate as a description of the origins of New York's elite.[32]

New York's plutocracy had as much wealth as did their European counterparts but could often live on the same baronial scale at less expense. During the height of the financial crisis of 1857, Strong could write that, "In Wall Street every man carries Pressure, Anxiety, Loss written on his forehead."[33] For the truly wealthy, the vicissitudes of the business cycle did not mean that much. Well-to-do men who did suffer business reverses, such as Strong's father-in-law, Samuel Ruggles, might recover and rebuild their fortunes. In short, in the expanding economy that was midcentury New York City the rich received a larger share of a growing pie. They could and did use this wealth to live sumptuously.[34]

Below the level of the families of great inherited wealth, successful business and professional men and their families had comfortable and gratifying lives. There were dinner, dancing, and sleighing parties, New Year's Day calls, performances of Mozart and Beethoven and the latest in Italian opera, and delicious and malicious gossip.[35] Conservative, older New Yorkers like Mordecai Noah might lament the passing of a simpler, more

intimate community; for the energetic and aggressive the burgeoning city of the 1850s offered a range of economic, cultural,
and recreational opportunities far beyond those of Knickerbocker New York.[36]

For those not so fortunate, New York's growth meant crowd-
ing, contentious disputes over jobs and housing, and susceptibil-
ity to disease and demoralization. New Yorkers of the early
nineteenth century did not look to government for solutions of
social problems beyond maintaining order and providing some
minimal relief. The predominant emotion associated with government was fear—fear of the abuse of political power. The rid-
icule that Irving's *History* directed at political figures reflected
a widespread hostility to politics and politicians. Even those
who held public office often shared this negative view of their
calling. In Washington, members of executive departments and
congressmen reinforced the structural separation between them
mandated by the Constitution in their living arrangements. Ex-
ecutives and congressmen lived at opposite ends of the city and
were conscious of crossing a gulf when they visited each
other.[37]

In New York City, the charter from 1830 on fragmented
power so that no individual or group could control the varied
reins of city government. The growing size and complexity of
city government led to the creation of new functions and new institutions, such as the Metropolitan Board of Health in 1866, but
only grudgingly and against considerable opposition. New departments often had considerable structural autonomy, so that
municipal government became a patchwork of independent
boards and commissions, each jealous of its own preserve and
resistant to central control. Men such as Fernando Wood, William Tweed, and John Kelly who tried to provide direction and
coordination were attacked as "usurpers" and "tyrants." Few
people seemed ready to believe that politicians could be trusted
and government used to promote social well-being, except in
carefully defined and limited ways. Many of their fears and cautions were justified; no one really knew how to administer effec-
tively a large and complex city.[38]

The cost, however, of giving the private sector free reign and allowing market mechanisms to allocate income and space without social controls was increased inequality and a deterioration of the quality of life for the less favored in comparison with conditions in Irving's youth. New York City made great progress between 1809 and 1859, but there was a high price tag attached.

Religion and Politics
in Knickerbocker Times

Joseph L. Blau

Washington Irving's father was a Presbyterian of a rigorous and stern cast, as befitted an American of Scottish descent. His mother, of English background, was sympathetic to the Episcopal Church. Irving himself was more deeply attracted to Episcopalianism than to Presbyterianism. With his mother's assistance, and contrary to his father's wishes, he attended theatrical performances and pursued other light amusements in his youth. Later, he was confirmed in the Episcopal Church. During his years in New York City, his religious affiliation seems not to have weighed heavily upon him. Later, however, in Tarrytown, he became much more deeply involved in the activities of his church. Thus Irving's own life illustrates two important features of religious life in New York State—its pluralism and its voluntary character.

These two qualities, eminently visible in New York and Pennsylvania, but present to a lesser degree in other states as well, were a major factor in determining the relation of politics and religion in late eighteenth-century and early nineteenth-century America. The notion of separation of church and state did not arise out of the meditations of any single individual or any group of theorists. In the first instance, separation was a practical device making it possible for people of diverse beliefs and unbeliefs to carry on their political affairs together even when they worshiped apart. Essential to the achievement of this objective was the drawing of proper boundaries between the spheres of secular affairs and religion.

This essay points out some New York examples of the kinds of questions that were agitated in the course of fixing these guidelines. I shall try briefly to recapitulate aspects of the story of the colonial period that are useful for understanding later developments and then to report these cases, ending with very limited conclusions.

Colonial New York is the classic instance of what is spoken of by historians of the relation of church and state as "multiple establishment." Originally, in the period of Dutch domination, New Netherland supported an established Dutch Reformed Church and tolerated the "private" practice of other denominational forms of worship, such as those of English Congregationalism and Presbyterianism. Soon the tolerated denominations were permitted to go "public," that is, to build their own church buildings. Other groups were not so fortunate. Lutherans, as well as the more usual Baptists and Quakers, were subject to prison sentences for holding worship services in private homes. The handful of Jews in New Amsterdam were permitted a cemetery, but no synagogue, although they too were allowed to conduct private worship.

When the British captured New Amsterdam in 1664 the position of special privilege of the Dutch Reformed Church was lost, but this did not imply separation of church and state. Instead, the Instructions of the Duke of York—sometimes referred to as "the Duke's laws"—extended the official concern for the maintenance of religious institutions to all Protestant denominations indifferently. Efforts during the 1680s to shift to a preferred status for the Church of England were successful in only four counties in the entire colony.

The widespread revulsion against institutional and established religion that culminated in the insistent clamor for the religious freedom clauses of the First Amendment to the Federal Constitution was reflected in New York by its 1777 state constitution. Here all existing laws that "may be construed to establish or maintain any particular denomination of Christians or their ministers" were declared null and void, and "free exercise and enjoyment of religious profession and worship without discrimina-

The Old Dutch Church, Sleepy Hollow, North Tarrytown, N.Y.,
founded in 1697 and now a National Historic Landmark.
This watercolor by William R. Miller (1818–1893) is dated
August 11, 1851, and shows a federal-style pillared porch since
removed. From the Library of Sleepy Hollow Restorations.

tion or preference" guaranteed in perpetuity. Thus New York State, even before Virginia—supposedly the bellwether of religious freedom—had introduced constitutional provisions for religious freedom. Possibly the often-discussed clause of this constitution and its early revisions excluding clergymen from civil office on the ground that they "ought not to be diverted from their great duties of the service of God and the cure of souls" was an indication of a fear that, if members of the clergy were to be elected to office, religious freedom would be a casualty.

Of course, some part of the opposition to political involvement in the support of religious institutions was affected by financial considerations. For the poor citizens of states hovering on the edge of bankruptcy, as were all the states for many years after the Revolution, public support of churches and ministers of religion would have been a costly luxury. Economical salvation rather than the "economy of salvation" had to be their central concern. Even the highly principled discussion of James Madison's *Memorial and Remonstrance on the Religious Rights of Man* was, in fact, directed against a bill before the Virginia legislature, the House of Burgesses, providing for payment of "teachers of religion" out of public funds. The successful efforts of Madison and others to prevent the passage of the assessment bill may have resulted as much from the financial concern of the Virginia legislators as from the cogency of Madison's 16 arguments.

In addition, we must also note that (unlike the situation today) church leaders of the eighteenth and early nineteenth centuries and their revivalistic contemporaries were frequently antagonistic to each other. The Second Great Awakening, beginning in the 1790s, lasted until about 1850. To some extent, as R. H. Gabriel has shown, its frontier revivalism penetrated deeply into the American political spirit because the revivalistic emphasis on the salvation of the individual soul through a personal conversion experience minimized the importance of the mediatorial role of institutions. Not surprisingly, the more revival-minded Protestants did not show great enthusiasm for state support of their formal churchly rivals. In Western New York State, under spur of Charles G. Finney's evangelistic thrust, the Awakening continued into the middle of the nineteenth century.

Frontier "enthusiastic" religion of this sort was not a once-a-week, every-week kind of religion; it was catch-as-catch-can. Whenever a circuit-riding preacher came within a reasonable distance, all work was halted for the duration of his stay. Whole families indulged in a prolonged orgy of emotional religiosity. Not all the emotion that was generated was religiously directed; Jonathan Edwards in his keen psychological analyses of the first Great Awakening had already pointed out that not all "raised affections" were "gracious affections." Revival time had all the atmosphere of carnival—noise, excitement, stimulation, contact with one's fellow human beings, the opportunity to laugh and to weep and also to feel again that one had cleared the account with God. In the starved lives of the frontier New Yorkers, revivalism served a religious purpose, and much more. But it did not build churches.

We should also note that among the Jeffersonian partisans in New York State (and especially in New York City) there was at least a small faction whose deistic beliefs accorded with those of Thomas Paine in seeing no need for any institutionalized religion. When Paine said, "My own mind is my own church," he gave expression to a form of religious individualism different from that of the frontier revivalists, but one that was equally anti-ecclesiastical. This extreme position is well represented in the writings of the blind former minister, Elihu Palmer, who composed the "Principles of the Deistical Society of the State of New York," which he helped organize in the 1790s. Later, there were even more explicitly free-thinking groups that flourished mildly in the open-minded urbanity of New York City. For example, Frances Wright and her associate Robert Dale Owen moved the Owenite *New-Harmony Gazette* from its communal home in Indiana to New York City and renamed the paper *The Free Enquirer*.

Each of these groups, for its own reasons, supported a separation of politics and religious life. Some were convinced that the only way to keep politics clean was to keep churches and their minions out of the state; at the other extreme were those who were convinced that the only way to keep religion pure was to keep politicians and their greedy hands out of religion. All were certain that the separation they advocated would operate for the ultimate advantage of both religious and political life in the United States.

Undeniably, separation worked to the immediate disadvantage of those churches that had been publicly supported in the colonial period. The newer position allowed no special advantage to accrue to any church, large or small. It gave no exceptional status—personal, civic, or economic—to those who were members of any church. It "established" not irreligion, as some overhasty opponents have claimed, but the "voluntary system." All Americans were free to choose to support the religious (or antireligious) group and the ministry that met their individual needs for spiritual guidance and sustenance. A church that could not gain the voluntary support of a substantial group of Americans could not maintain itself. There was no privileged church that could afford to be insensitive to the religious needs of the people. Every church had to satisfy its potential adherents in order to earn their support. Even though it may be somewhat shocking to us with our overdone fear of giving offense to anyone, I feel the best description of the ideal for religion on the American scene was that of the Jacksonian journalist, William Leggett, who spoke, in a New York *Plaindealer* editorial in 1836, of *"perfect free trade in religion—*of leaving it to manage its own concerns in its own way, without government protection, regulation, or interference of any kind or degree whatever."

Needless to say, issues arose in the first half of the nineteenth century that involved efforts to draw the line between legitimate and illegitimate relations of religion and politics, even though the general principle was widely accepted. Was it, for example, an unwarranted state action to exclude ministers from the holding of elective office, as was done by the New York State Constitution of 1777 and also the revision of 1821? Enough people considered this prohibition undesirable to eliminate the restrictive clause in the Revised Statutes of 1829. Clearly in this instance there was an illegitimate extension of the principle of separation in that a religious "test act" was applied to restrict the civil rights of some individuals.

Not only the New York State Constitution, but also the Constitution of the United States prohibited test acts. In the 1820s the question was raised whether this prohibition precluded any inquiry into the religious beliefs of a candidate for office. After all, Jefferson had been publicly attacked for his religious beliefs during the campaign of 1800; and Alexander Hamilton, at about the same time, had suggested in a private letter that a concerted effort by religionists might be desirable to avert the election of an antagonist of religion. In 1827 Ezra Stiles Ely, a leading Presbyterian minister, delivered in Philadelphia a sermon entitled "The Duty of Christian Freemen to Elect Christian Rulers" in which he raised the entire question of the utility of such a pre-election unofficial "test act." The context was the forthcoming election of 1828, and from the standpoint of an orthodox churchman there was good reason for concern. Of the six men who had been elected to the presidency between 1788 and 1824, none could by the remotest stretch of the imagination have been regarded as an orthodox Protestant Christian, though all were nominal members of one or another Christian church. All the members of the "Virginia dynasty" professed deistic beliefs while the father and son from Massachusetts supported the developing Unitarian movement. It is not to be marveled at that leaders like Ely were beginning to chafe, and to wonder when a *real* Christian would have a turn at the presidential office!

Ely suggested a way in which the orthodoxy, or at least the ostensible orthodoxy, of the president-elect could be guaranteed. His proposal was that voters who were members of the seven Protestant denominations to which he was willing to concede the title "orthodox" should constitute themselves unofficially as an intersectarian pressure group to prevent the election of "opponents of Christianity" to governmental office. This group he called "a Christian party in politics." He was shrewd enough to see that his program might well promote hypocrisy, but this did not bother him. He was concerned with the appearance of orthodoxy, not its actuality. "It is a matter of thankfulness," he argued, if candidates for office "are constrained to SEEM such persons." His logic was astounding. The fact that "infidels" had been elected proved that they had been put into office by the votes of fellow-infidels; why, then, should "Christians" not follow the same practice? "Are Christians the only men in the community who may not be guided by their judgment, conscience, and choice in electing their rulers?"

This proposal, which was printed and given wide distribution, inevitably stirred up resentment and controversy. Part of the ferment of the early years of the Jacksonian era in New York centered in the discussion of Ely's suggestion. Frances Wright, with her gift for vigorous and pointed controversy, must be awarded the palm for the most interesting and liveliest reply, in the *Free Enquirer,* picturing what America might be like under the regime of Ely's "Christian party in politics":

> Washington carried by storm; a Baptist senate; a Methodist House of Representatives; an Episcopalian cabinet and a Presbyterian president! And to perfect the odor of sanctity of this New-Jerusalem upon earth, you must imagine a Supreme Court, compounded of Bishops, Presbyters, Elders, Deacons, and high-seat Fathers of double-refined orthodoxy, propounding the soundest theology of all the sound churches, and trying every case, domestic and foreign, national, international, and individual, by the church catechism, the thirty-nine articles, the Westminster confession of faith, the apostles' creed and the revelations of the apocalypse.

Another issue that involved determination of boundaries between the proper spheres of religion and politics—an issue that was explicitly raised in the New York State legislature—was whether the hiring of chaplains to open legislative sessions with prayer breached the wall of separation. To most of us today this seems a trivial issue. Yet, only a few years before the question came up in New York State, legislative chaplains were first appointed to open the sessions of Congress in Washington. James Madison did not approve. In 1822, in a letter to Edward Livingston, Madison wrote

> . . . I observe with particular pleasure the view you have taken of the immunity of Religion from civil jurisdiction, in every case where it does not trespass on private rights or the public peace. This has always been a favorite principle with me; and it was not with my approbation, that the deviation from it took place in Congress, when they appointed Chaplains, to be paid from the National Treasury. It would have been a much better proof to their Constituents of their pious feeling if the members had contributed for the purpose, a pittance from their own pockets. . . .

Further, in an essay left in manuscript and not published until 1914, Madison argued explicitly that the appointment of chaplains violates the Constitution by establishing a national religion and is also inconsistent with "the pure principle of religious freedom."

When New York's Revised Statutes were issued in 1829, they provided for the payment of legislative chaplains, thus violating the state constitution. As soon as this overriding of the fundamental law of the state became widely known, the legislature received petitions and memorials from all sections of the state protesting the legislative chaplaincies. In 1832, some 26 petitions were received by the state assembly. In 1833, on the first four days of the session, no fewer than 22 memorials came to the assembly, and others to the state senate. Among the counties from which such protests were sent were: Dutchess, Tompkins, New York, Onondaga, Greene, Allegany, Orange, Genesee, Albany, and Columbia. I have not visited the State Archives to try to recover the full list; in the assembly records, the clerk's entry sometimes took the form: "Ten several memorials of sundry inhabitants of this state. . . ." Also from the bare record it is not possible to tell what the objections were. It may well have been the case that most protests were directed against *paying* legislative chaplains, not explicitly against *having* them.

At all events, a resolution was proposed at the opening session of the assembly in 1832: That the clerk of the House request the several clergymen of Albany having charge of congregations to attend the House each morning to open its deliberations by prayer. By what certainly seems like prearrangement, this commonplace resolution was tabled. On the following day, David Moulton, Assemblyman from Oneida County, moved an amendment that required [!] the clergymen to serve without compensation. Amendment defeated, 85 to 36. John C. Kemble, Assemblyman from Rensselaer County, moved to amend by providing for assessment of the members of the House to pay for the ministers' service. Defeated by, needless to say, an even greater margin, 96 to 28. Original resolution then passed without recorded vote.

Later, Moulton and Kemble, proposers of these tongue-in-cheek amendments, were named with Mordecai Myers of New York County as a "select committee" to consider the various petitions and to bring before the House a report on the whole question of legislative chaplaincies. The report is a good statement of the negative case, but the resolutions suggested by the authors were tabled and never acted upon. In the next session, 1833, when the resolution to appoint chaplains was proposed, Dudley Burwell, Assemblyman from Herkimer County, moved that it be referred to the "Select committee to which was referred sundry memorials for a repeal of the law compensating legislative chaplains." In 1833, this committee consisted of Thomas Herttell of New York County, a leader in the freethought groups of the period, and Ichabod C. Baker of Oneida County, an avowed opponent of the chaplaincies, together with Charles Rogers of Washington County, who was known to be in favor of having chaplains. Had Burwell's motion to refer to this committee been passed, the appointment of chaplains would have been a dead issue for that session. It did not pass, though the vote was close; the defeat was by a vote of 67 to 54. Then

Isaac Van Duzer of Orange County proposed the following amendment to the original resolution: "That the members of this House contribute and pay for such services, such sum or compensation as they may see fit." Once again this attempt to make politicians pay for their own presumed spiritual solace was defeated by a larger margin (71 to 50), and the original resolution then passed, 80 to 40.

If this action brought any joy to those who advocated legislative chaplaincies, a group of 13 Protestant ministers soon transformed that joy into mortification by their refusal of the invitation:

> The undersigned have carefully considered the subject connected with this invitation and in view of the opposition which the employment of chaplains by the Legislature has met with within a few years past; the unpleasant discussion which it has occasioned, and which will probably be renewed from year to year; they believe *they* will best subserve the interests of religion by respectfully declining the invitation of the Honorable the Senate and Assembly.

Only a day or two later, Assemblyman Dudley Burwell introduced a bill to repeal the section of the Revised Statutes of 1829 that provided for the payment of legislative chaplains. Both the assembly and the senate voted affirmatively on this measure. Thus a compromise was reached that did not put the legislature on record on the question of principle, but did eliminate, for the time being, what so many of the petitioners considered an improper use of public funds.

I do not wish to editorialize or to sermonize on these indications of a great concern in the first half of the nineteenth century, in New York State and in other states, to maintain a proper distinctness of secular and religious affairs. My purpose has been more to show, first, that the multiplicity of religious (and antireligious) groups in New York State, a larger number than in any other state with the exception of Pennsylvania, was a major factor in keeping religion out of politics and state politics out of religion. Second, I believe I have shown that public political professions of piety, commonplace as they have become in today's United States, were resented and protested not merely by the urban "sophisticates" of New York City but also by the "honest yeomen" of the rural areas of the state. Finally, I suggest that if we would understand the New York—and the America—of Washington Irving's day, we must recognize that the persistent eighteenth-century distrust of the *agents* of institutional religion ("priestcraft") was strengthened and confirmed by the evangelical distrust of the *agencies* of institutional religion, especially distrust of the political aims of settled churches.

The standard history of the relation between religion and politics in New York State is Sanford H. Cobb, *The Rise of Religious Liberty in America* (New York: Macmillan, 1902), especially pp. 303ff. More recent accounts—dependent, however, largely on Cobb—may be found in Anson Phelps Stokes, *Church and State in the United States* (New York: Harper and Brothers, 1950), and Leo Pfeffer, *Church, State and Freedom* (Boston: Beacon Press, 1953), both of which emphasize the legal and constitutional history of the question.

Many of the documents of the earlier period are reprinted with interpretation and general commentary in Joseph L. Blau, ed., *Cornerstones of Religious Freedom in America* (Boston: Beacon Press, 1949); this includes the most available text of Madison's "Memorial and Remonstrance," pp. 81–87. The texts of charter and constitutional provisions and legislative enactments of both the Colonial and the Early National periods are collected in F. N. Thorpe, *The Federal and State Constitutions, Colonial Charters and Other Organic Laws* (Washington, D. C.: Government Printing Office, 1909).

For the New York story as it applies to the Jews of the Colonial Period, see Abram V. Goodman, *American Overture* (Philadelphia: Jewish Publication Society of America, 1947) and documents in the early pages of Morris U. Schappes, *A Documentary History of the News in the United States, 1654–1875*, 3rd ed. (New York: Schocken Books, 1971).

There are a number of good historical surveys of the history of religion in the United States, all of which discuss the Early National Period and the impact of the Second Great Awakening. Ralph H. Gabriel, *The Course of American Democratic Thought*, 2nd ed. (New York: The Ronald Press Company, 1956) best states the contribution of the revivalistic forms of Protestantism to the development of democratic thought and institutions.

Among the many monographs dealing with the revivalism of the early nineteenth century, Whitney R. Cross, *The Burnt-Over District: The Social and Intellectual History of Enthusiastic*

Religion in Western New York, 1800–1850 (Ithaca, N. Y.: Cornell University Press, 1950) is outstanding. There are valuable insights, too, in Charles C. Cole, Jr., *The Social Ideas of the Northern Evangelists, 1826–1860* (New York: Columbia University Press, 1954).

The central importance of pluralism and voluntarism to the shaping of American attitudes has been excitingly developed by Sidney E. Mead, *The Lively Experiment* (New York: Harper and Row, 1963). There have been valuable studies of the radical free-thought movements of the Early National Period by G. Adolf Koch, *Republican Religion: the American Revolution and the Age of Reason* (New York: Henry Holt & Co.. 1933), and by Albert Post, *Popular Freethought in America, 1825–1850* (New York: Columbia University Press, 1943).

Much of the material discussed in this brief presentation rests on my own researches, some published in various articles or included in anthologies I have edited, and some unpublished. For those who would wish more detail, I list here (in addition to *Cornerstones of Religious Freedom in America,* which contains the full text of the "Moulton-Myers Report" as well as some responses to Ezra Stiles Ely), the following articles: "The Freeborn Mind," *Review of Religion,* IX (1944), 31–41; "The Christian Party in Politics," *Review of Religion,* XI (1946), 18–35; and "Freedom of Prayer," *Review of Religion,* XIV (1950), 250–69.

Political Satire
in Knickerbocker's *History*

Michael L. Black

In 1819 AND 1820, while the seven numbers of *The Sketch Book* were being read, praised, and even reprinted first in America and then in Great Britain, one critic compared the Diedrich Knickerbocker of 1809 to the Geoffrey Crayon of 1819 and decided that, on the whole, 1809 had been the better year:

> He appears to have lost a little of that natural run of style, for which his lighter writings were so remarkable. . . . It is as if his mother England had been sent abroad to be improved, and in attempting to become accomplished, had lost too many of her home qualities. . . . The fact is, that what is idiomatic and essentially English—that which is in us and a part of us from old and familiar associations, and on which, too, the eye can rest as upon a picture,—has been laid aside for a language which is learned like a foreign one, and which must always be wanting to us, in some degree, in character, definiteness and nearness.[1]

This American critic, Richard Henry Dana, was not the only reader who preferred Knickerbocker; so did John Gibson Lockhart, one of the most important British critics of the time.[2] And the leading British publisher, John Murray, who had published *The Sketch Book* when the original British publisher went bankrupt, wrote the author that *A History of New York* was "your opus magnum."[3]

They praised a work that was radically different from *The*

Sketch Book, for Knickerbocker's *History* is, among other things, a lampoon on European histories, European epics, American politics, American windiness and braggadocio, New England tricksters, and New York torpor. It is also a history of New York, faithful to what was known in 1809 of the general outline of events in the Dutch province of New Netherland discovered by Henry Hudson in 1609 and surrendered to the British by Peter Stuyvesant in 1664. Nevertheless, the author freely and frequently invents anecdotes, characters, and events because he lacked historical data, or because he wanted to make New Amsterdam a seventeenth-century version of the New York of 1809, or because he wanted to show his skill as a writer.

Even after the major revisions of 1812 and 1848 and the minor revision of 1819, 1824, and 1829, Knickerbocker's *History* retains much of the gusto of the first edition of 1809. This Knickerbocker—the author of "Rip Van Winkle," "The Legend of Sleepy Hollow," and other stories is not the same persona—but a lost child of the eighteenth century. As in *Gulliver's Travels* and numerous other works, the author's manuscript is actually published by someone else, the owner of a hotel where the author has been staying, who swears that the manuscript is genuine and that the author really exists. The author then introduces himself in the section "To the Public."

One-seventh of the *History,* Book I, isn't history at all but a long preface about the creation of the world, the peopling of America, and the legality of the discoverers' action, to which is attached, as an analogy, a hypothetical conquest of the earth by moon men. In Book II, Hudson inadvertently discovers New York, and the broad-bottomed Dutch colonize the New World in the round-bottomed *Goede Vrouw,* settling first on the west bank of the Hudson River at Communipaw before most of them remove to New Amsterdam. In Book III, the colony gets its first governor and its first threat; Wouter Van Twiller dozes and snores through a prosperous administration in which his only official action is a Solomon-like decision in a lawsuit; he dies in the middle of the siege of Fort Goed Hoop on the Connecticut River. The fort falls at the start of the troubled reign of William

A satiric illustration by Charles R. Leslie (1794–1859), for the
London edition in 1821 of Knickerbocker's *History of New York,*
later separately issued by the publisher. Courtesy of New-York
Historical Society.

In the first edition of 1809 Irving wrote, of Governor Kieft,
"It is incredible how the little governor chuckled at beholding
caitiff vagrants and sturdy beggars thus swinging by the
breech, and cutting gambols in the air."

Kieft in Book IV; the bustling ways and "universal acquire-
ments" of William the Testy produce one military victory over
the Yankees at Oyster Bay and introduce political factions to the
colony.

In Books V-VII, Knickerbocker's hero Peter Stuyvesant battles the Yankees, the Swedes on the Delaware, and his own subjects. The first campaign is inconclusive, but at the great battle
of Fort Christina, his forces conquer all New Sweden. King
Charles II ends the Dutch hegemony when he sends a British
fleet to conquer New Amsterdam. The hardheaded governor
finds his fellow Dutchmen eager to hand the colony over to the
enemy; and he finally agrees to a capitulation, after which he
retires to his farm or *Bouwery* to live out his days in patriarchal style.

This is a rough summary of the most historically accurate of
the several editions, the 1809 edition. However, it provides little
idea of the richness of the work. If the work was begun as
"nothing more . . . than a temporary jeu d'esprit," as Irving half
apologized in the 1848 edition,[4] it turned out to be a permanent
exercise of wit. Like the narrator of Henry Fielding's *Tom
Jones*, Irving's narrator interrupts the narrative, but his philoso-
phizing is closer to that of Walter Shandy in Laurence Sterne's
Tristram Shandy. Knickerbocker's effusions on the past parody
the sentimental mooning of some of his contemporaries over de-
cayed ruins; he contributes learned footnotes which appear spu-
rious but which are quite accurate; he scatters classical allusions
throughout his work. Today's readers, products of a culture in
which knowledge has greatly diffused and expanded, do not
perceive Homer, Rabelais, Cervantes, Shakespeare, Swift, and
Sterne as the living presences they were for Irving in 1809; now
they are writers read in college or entries in reference books.
Thus much of Irving's wit, when it has been explained, seems
more learned than it really is.

In good eighteenth-century fashion, Knickerbocker's *History*
appeals to the head, not the heart. So does *Salmagundi*, which
delighted New York in 1807 and 1808. Much of Knickerbocker's
closest literary relative seems labored and tedious, however: an

attack upon the American poetaster Thomas Green Fessenden, several "Stranger" essays parodying the style of the popular British writer Edward Carr, and the recurrent guffaws about the works of the historian Linkum Fidelius. Even the best pieces in *Salmagundi,* such as some of the letters from the Tripolitan captive Mustapha or Linkum's account of the Hoppingtots' capture of the city of Gotham, pale beside the description of Wouter Van Twiller ("a robustious beer barrel standing on skids"), the economical measures of William the Testy for battling the Yankees, or the superb mock-epic battle between Stuyvesant's Dutch and Risingh's Swedes at Fort Christina, with its Homeric catalogue of warriors, intervention of deities, and single combat between the Dutch Achilles and the Swedish Hector. *Salmagundi* cannot be dislodged from its time and place, but Knickerbocker's *History* has carried its heavy encumbrance of literary and local jokes easily.

Any attempt to classify the volumes in the Author's Revised Edition will show that Knickerbocker is odd man out: four sketch books (*The Sketch Book, Bracebridge Hall, Tales of a Traveller,* and *Wolfert's Roost*); three Western books (*A Tour on the Prairies, Astoria,* and *Adventures of Captain Bonneville*); two Spanish works (*The Conquest of Granada* and *The Alhambra*); four romantic biographies (*Columbus and The Companions of Columbus, Oliver Goldsmith, Mahomet and His Successors,* and *George Washington*); and two long descriptive essays (*Abbotsford* and *Newstead Abbey*).[5]

Irving nevertheless included this raucous display of eighteenth-century wit among the politely emotional and the really historical products of his long career, expressing the hope that Diedrich Knickerbocker's book would "still be received with good-humored indulgence and be thumbed and chuckled over by the family fireside."[6] Mid-Victorian American received the book just this way, and so did later generations as critics shouted themselves hoarse with praise for the first American fireside writer. After 70 years as a republic, only months after a successful war with Mexico, amid talk of the nation's Manifest Destiny, America needed a great writer. Thus Irving became the first American classic, the first fireside writer. Every work, revised or new, that he published from 1848 to his death in 1859 as part of his collected edition was received eagerly, particularly his greatly expanded biography of Oliver Goldsmith and his five-volume biography of George Washington. In contrast to 1824, when he had been accused of offending "the chastity of the Georgian home" in parts of *Tales of a Traveller*,[7] he was welcomed into the purity of the Victorian home in 1848.

Sets of Irving's works became necessary knickknacks in the nineteenth-century American home, but all too frequently the volumes seem not to have been read or the pages cut open. Knickerbocker's *History*, Irving's most popular work,[8] continued to retain improprieties such as a reference to a scatological poem attributed to Swift, passages on bundling, an obscene Dutch oath, a reference to a flatulent dragon, and the double meaning of Antony Van Corlear's trumpet that had delighted "the strapping wenches of New England."[9] No other American author was permitted such liberties in the 1840s, as Melville learned when he had to revise *Typee*.[10] Irving, however, was not condemned.

The indecencies mentioned above—and there are others—[11] stayed in Knickerbocker's *History* for nearly 40 years, from the first edition of 1809 to the final edition of 1848.[12] They are still there, delighting and surprising readers and critics who have begun to hustle Knickerbocker away from the fireside into a more appropriate room. Some have discovered more of Irving's historical and literary sources;[13] others, led by William L. Hedges in his excellent study of all of Irving's work from *Jonathan Oldstyle* in 1802–03 through *The Alhambra* in 1832, have discussed Knickerbocker's ideas about history and his skill as a writer.[14] Source-hunting, a function of "scholarship," and literary analysis, a function of "criticism," can be united by considering *A History of New York* as a provincial work that has become universal and a timely work of 1809 that has become timeless. Some parts of the political and literary worlds of 1809 and some indication of Irving's use of these parts as an artist can be gained by reaching into the *History* to comment on two char-

acters, William Kieft and General Von Poffenburgh, and by staying outside the text itself to comment on the circumstances in
which the book was first published.

The most obvious use of the political world of 1809 is the connection of William Kieft, the second of Knickerbocker's three
Dutch governors, to Thomas Jefferson, whose two terms as President had ended in March 1809, only eight months before *A History of New York* appeared. Forty years later, Irving revised
the *History* extensively—particularly Book IV, which covers the
reign of William the Testy—and in the process he removed
many of the similarities between the character and the President.
Since the 1848 edition is the one which most readers know,[15]
they should realize that the revised Kieft is not a caricature of
Jefferson. Many of the 1809 parallels between the governor and
the President do remain: Kieft is a man of science, although his
many inventions are dismissed as "wrong–headed contriv-
ances;"[16] he defends the colony against Yankee squatting on the
Connecticut River by proclamations, as Jefferson, according to
his opponents, defended the nation against British, French, and
Spanish indignities by proclamation;[17] when the Dutch governor's words are not heeded, he orders nonintercourse with the
Yankees.[18] Finally, following his "unfortunate propensity . . .
[for] experiment and innovations," the people become interested in politics and form three parties, the aristocratic Long
Pipes (Federalists), the plebeian Short Pipes (Democratic-
Republicans), and Quids (the name of John Randolph's faction in 1809).[19] However, the two chapters about Killian Van
Rensellaer's challenge to the governor's authority are new in
1848 and refer to the 1830s Anti-Rent controversy in New York,[20]
and the introduction of Kieft's plan to use seawant or wampum
as currency recalls the financial disorder of the 1830s.[21]

To see how skillfully and extensively Irving satirizes the third
President of the United States, one has to read an earlier edition
of *A History of New York*. One might as well return to the
first edition, since the political world of 1809 is best represented
there. The original Book IV contains so many dated jokes and
references that the political satire could easily sink in a sea of

learned—and essential—footnotes. For example, Knickerbocker can remark that his fellow citizens of 1809 do not complain about infringements of their rights, a broad allusion which could have included the President's interference in the trial of Aaron Burr in 1807,[22] but when an American sailor ("The unlucky Pierce") is killed by a British ship, suddenly "the whole body politic [is] in a ferment."[23] Yet, aside from the reference to an 1806 coastal incident, the modern reader needs no further information; in fact, the reference to the particular ship may even have detracted the attention of Irving's first readers from the point about the public's misplaced energies.[24]

The popularity of Knickerbocker's *History*, long after Jefferson had become an American political saint, is certainly not a result of readers' knowledge of Irving's political satire. Indeed, most readers have been unaware of the caricature, not because of their lack of knowledge but because of Irving's skill as a satirist. Had he sprinkled his text with too many of the very specific references like the one above, Irving would have written another *Salmagundi*, which needed a decent set of explanatory notes by 1860.

Irving made the specific into the universal in something like Swift's manner in *Gulliver's Travels*. When Gulliver awakens among the Lilliputians, Swift transmutes the petty squabbles of the English court of the early eighteenth century into a double-sided coin: on the obverse is a story; on the reverse is a satire. That we no longer see both sides of the coin without some explanation is not so important as the fact that, ignorant of the personalities referred to, we can see that their actions are meant to be typical of all men in all ages. The qualification for political preferment is not statesmanship but acrobatics on a metaphorical tightrope;[25] political parties can be seen to be no different from men in high heels and men in low heels;[26] those who refuse to follow orders "to force the consciences, or destroy the liberties of an innocent people" are called traitors.[27]

In the same way, Knickerbocker's presentation of William the Testy becomes much more than an antiquated piece of anti-Jeffersonian pamphleteering. Kieft is Jefferson, and New Netherland is the United States of 1809, but Knickerbocker's presentation of both the Dutch governor and those he rules is one of the most incisive satirical comments on American politics ever written. Irving's vision is not as universal as Swift's because—to mention two important reasons—he is not as cynical about humanity (Irving was a product not of the age of neoclassicism but of the age of sensibility—and he had not held high position and then been turned out, like Swift), nor does he have Swift's all-encompassing conservatism. He is, however, able to step away from contemporary political broils and find recurrent themes and emphases in the contemporary world. When he satirizes Jeffersonian defense policies, which, in addition to a minuscule standing army, included a navy filled with light, inexpensive, and ineffectual gunboats,[28] he points to that long-lasting inattention to the nation's sea power that changed only when Manifest Destiny was transformed into the extracontinental land grabs of the 1890s. Irving's concern was immediate and local: in 1809, New York harbor was an inviting, and unfortified, target, as its citizens yelled for protection. Kieft uses "economy" as the "grand political *cabalistic word*"[29] to justify his policies, as did Jefferson, but it was economy that kept America's ports undefended, and it was economy that permitted land frauds and land speculation. In short, economy, a result of the Jeffersonian theory that the best government is one which governs least, may have been inimical to the nation's best interests.

Another part of the political world of New Netherland is Jacobus Von Poffenburgh, the commander-in-chief of the armies of the colony. The general, a hero of the fall of Fort Goed Hoop to the Yankees, was a favorite of Kieft, who listened for hours to "his gunpowder narratives of surprising victories—he never gained." Stuyvesant sends him to the Delaware River to defend against the encroaching Swedes, and the general erects Fort Casimer on the river. The Swedes protest, but Von Poffenburgh struts about his new fort, easing his spleen by carving up pumpkins as if they were Yankees, and disciplining an old veteran for refusing to obey orders. His fort falls to the Swedes when their leader Risingh pretends friendship and lands a party of men outside the fort. He flatters Von Poffenburgh into permitting him to inspect the fort, and the two commanders exhibit their troops' mastery of military tactics. The general, a great feeder and drinker, invites the Swedish commander to dinner, and when all the Dutch have passed out, the Swedes kick them out of the fort. A vagabond carries the true story of the fall of Fort Casimer to Stuyvesant, who refuses to accept the general's version and dismisses him.

Von Poffenburgh is Irving's satirical portrait of General James Wilkinson, commander-in-chief of the United States Army in 1809.[30] Irving watched Wilkinson's arrival in the Richmond, Virginia, courtroom to testify against Aaron Burr for treason, and he described that scene to James Kirke Paulding, with whom he was collaborating on *Salmagundi*.[31] He also knew that Samuel Swartwout, a Burr accomplice from New York City whom he knew, had taunted and jostled the obese Jeffersonian hero on the main street of Richmond, demanded a duel, and received no answer.[32] Wilkinson's size, his pompous statements, his consumption of food and alcohol, and his repeated pleas for more money were frequent subjects of newspaper and congressional remarks, as were rumors of his being a double agent for Spain, or even Great Britain.[33] In spite of numerous investigations, courts of inquiry, and a few court-martial, Wilkinson, who was of course tried by his own junior officers, was never found guilty of spying or any other serious charge, although he was indeed in the pay of the Spanish enemies he was supposed to be controlling on the southwestern frontier.[34]

Irving wrote that Burr had shown only " 'a slight expression of contempt . . . such as you would show on regarding any person to whom you were indifferent, but whom you considered mean and contemptible'."[36] In the *History*, Knickerbocker is not indifferent to Von Poffenburgh, nor does he consider him "mean and contemptible." Although the general is compared to More of More-hall who slew the famous flatulent dragon and a medieval knight "in the delectable romance of Pierce Forest" who proved his power and courage by belaboring the trees in a nearby forest, the most noticeable literary parallel is Falstaff, another swaggerer, swearer, and sot.[36] Von Poffenburgh is too stupid to be mean and too absurd to be contemptible.

Knickerbocker relates one anecdote about the general which seems too ridiculous to have any connection to Wilkinson's career. Von Poffenburgh, "in the course of his devout researches in the bible, (for the pious Eneas himself, could not exceed him in outward religion)," discovers the story of Absalom and promptly orders all his troops to shave off their beloved queues.[37] One old veteran, Kildermeester, refuses to comply and is court-martialled and convicted of insubordination. Before he can be punished, he dies of a fever, but he has arranged to be buried in a coffin with a well-placed knothole through which the queue dangles in triumph.[38]

The Kildermeester incident seems too outrageous to be real, and Knickerbocker relates the incident so well that it looks like a well-constructed fiction. Yet on April 30, 1801, Jefferson's commander-in-chief had ordered every soldier to cut his hair. One veteran of the Revolutionary War, Colonel Thomas Butler, one of the very few career officers in the pea-sized Army, refused to comply, and at first Wilkinson exempted him from the order. In 1803, however, he ordered Butler to comply, added charges of dereliction of duty, and arranged for a court-martial far from Butler's frontier post. The court decided merely to reprimand the old veteran, and Wilkinson was outraged. In February 1804, still with his hair, Butler was ordered to New Orleans by Wilkinson, and he learned in December that he would stand military trial again. The second court-martial sentenced him to a year's suspension, but the old colonel's death from yellow fever made the verdict moot.[39]

All Knickerbocker does, then, is exaggerate an incident in Wilkinson's incredible career, a court-martial which delighted those who hated the general and his civilian commander and which aroused controversy about his competence as America's commander-in-chief.[40] The Kildermeester-Butler story is the most detailed parallel between Von Poffenburgh and Wilkinson that Irving wrote. Another connection, a less certain one, is the loss of Fort Casimer to the Swedes and Wilkinson's behavior on

the Sabine River. On the southwestern frontier in the first years
of the nineteenth century, Wilkinson was unable to remove
Spanish garrisons which continued to remain along the Sabine
River in eastern Texas, although the United States thought the
area was part of the recently purchased Louisiana Territory. Although few shots were fired, the Spaniards remained, and because Wilkinson called the campaign a victory, he earned himself the derisive title "the hero of the Sabine."[41]

Although one of the parallels between Knickerbocker's Von
Poffenburgh and America's Wilkinson is definite and the other is
open to doubt and especially to further inquiry, everything
about Jacobus Von Poffenburgh has been thumbed and chuckled over for more than a century not because most readers
have understood the political satire but because Von Poffenburgh is one of Irving's greatest comic characters, an American
miles gloriosus.[42]

Irving's skill in creating the character also solved a potentially
serious conflict of artistic unity and historical necessity. Von Poffenburgh enters the *History* too late; he belongs in Book IV,
with Jefferson-Kieft, because of the Jefferson-Wilkinson relationship and because, like Kieft, his battles are fought on paper.
However, Irving introduces him at the end of Book V, in the
reign of Peter Stuyvesant. His appearance as army commander
is sudden, as in Knickerbocker's relation of how happy Kieft had
been with him.[43] The historian does what he can to explain why
Stuyvesant entrusts the command of the southern frontier to
him: there is no competitor and any other appointee would be
the general's junior, "a breach of military etiquette."[44] The explanation is somewhat awkward, but Irving refused to shift the fall
of Fort Casimer in 1654 into Kieft's reign, which he knew had
ended seven years earlier in 1647.[45] By keeping Knickerbocker's
History historical—and Irving seldom falsified the little historical data that he had—the author was able to create his own version of Stuyvesant's real southern campaign. Even though Von
Poffenburgh serves as a foil for Stuyvesant, a copper captain
versus a genuine one, and even though the Wilkinson caricature
is dismissed from service by his new commander, Stuyvesant's

acceptance of the general marks him as more thick-headed than hard-headed. Since Hard-koppig Piet, like Don Quixote, often trusts other frauds, especially the Amphyctionic Council at Boston,[46] the Von Poffenburgh incidents may help the reader see the double meaning in "Hard-koppig Piet."

Since Irving had no historical information whatsoever about the Dutch commander on the Delaware, he could have spared himself the artistic problems mentioned above simply by removing the character. Instead, the rapidity with which Von Poffenburgh enters the narrative and departs (or rather disappears) after his dismissal and the length of his stay all suggest that Irving inserted the character some time after he had decided on the book's basic arrangement. Nevertheless, he wanted to caricaturize James Wilkinson, and with some strain and more craft he got the character into the narrative. But was he correct in omitting another Wilkinson story he had referred to in his first draft? There the general is named *Snoever* ("braggart" in Dutch); the change to Von Poffenburgh in the printed version is both a linguistic accommodation to non-Knickerbockers and a use of "puffing" which had been attached to Wilkinson by others,[47] but Irving omitted an anecdote dating back to the Revolution. After the Battle of Saratoga in 1777, where the 20-year-old Wilkinson had performed very well as an aide to General Gates, he had been entrusted with the official report by the victorious Gates and ordered to deliver it to the Continental Congress, then sitting at York, Pennsylvania. Wilkinson paused for a time in Easton to visit his fiancée, and he arrived a week after the battle had been decided. He also arrived after an unofficial report had calmed the jittery members of Congress, and his tardiness prompted one member to suggest that he be awarded a pair of leaden spurs, not the customary medal or sword.[48] The remark may be apocryphal, but Congress kept no detailed records of its floor proceedings; all we know is that the anecdote became another one of the anti-Wilkinson comments found in anti-Jefferson newspapers about 1807.[49] Had Irving used this Wilkinson story, however, he would have decreased his concentration on the general's recent conduct, which interested the readers of

1809 more than an old story about the Revolution. What is more, the Butler court-martial better fitted the caricature of a military commander blown up by a sense of his own importance.

The brilliant caricature of Wilkinson, however, succeeds at first as personal, not political satire. With no knowledge of who Wilkinson was or what he did, the modern reader may see political satire, however, particularly if he has heard of Jefferson's antipathy towards a standing army. Von Poffenburgh, that is, could be seen as a realization of a Republican slogan. The real James Wilkinson was not stupid or absurd; he was indeed a mean and contemptible (and fascinating) man, a schemer, a liar, a coward, a bully, and a traitor. Yet Knickerbocker presents him as a witless Falstaff, an act of pure satirical charity. It is certainly an act of political charity, and Jacobus Von Poffenburgh and James Wilkinson have survived as relatively unknown doubles.

At the very young age of 26, Irving proved himself to be one of the best writers of American political satire, a genre that has not flourished in this country. He portrayed Thomas Jefferson as a learned bumbler, but the real attack is on the President's philosophy of government and what it does to the New Netherlanders: defend the province only with words and change the peaceful Dutchmen into political partisans. Compare the shrillness of Philip Roth's *Our Gang*, an attack not on Nixonianism but on President Nixon. With General James Wilkinson, Irving does something different: makes the character so ridiculous that his real-life counterpart ought to be regarded as a serious threat.

All this is presented with remarkable spirit and dash, and Irving continued this spirit when he slapped the local historical society in the face, published Knickerbocker's *History* at the most insulting time possible, and orchestrated a two-part literary hoax. As Irving created a local and a literary atmosphere for his book, he also revealed his attitudes toward collectors of historical antiquities and literature itself.

Kickerbocker dedicates his work to the New-York Historical

Society, "as humble and unworthy Testimony of [his] profound veneration and exalted esteem."[50] The Society had been organized in 1804, but by October 1809, when Irving became a member, it had been unable to instill in New Yorkers a serious concern for "the natural, civil, literary, and ecclesiastical history of our country, and particularly of the State of New York. . . ."[51] New York, like most of the rest of America in 1809, was too busy growing in the present and thinking of the future to be bothered with the past. All the other original colonies and even some states admitted to the Union after 1789 had had their history related in accounts that met contemporary standards of historiography, but not New York. One reason was that the Dutch had been the first settlers and had decided to keep all their colonial records in the only language they knew. Over 50 years of Dutch rule occupy a mere nine pages of William Smith's *The History of the Province of New-York* (1757); the events and records of the 1664 surrender, covering less than three months, occupy 13 pages.[52] Smith's work was the standard authority in 1809 because it was the only authority in English, and Irving had no choice but to use it.

New York deserved a fuller account of its Dutch background, and some of the Society's published queries in 1805 concerned the Dutch colony. One of them shows how little was known:

Is there any thing known concerning *Wouter Van Twiller,* or *William Kieft,* who preceded Governor *Stuyvesant* in the Chief Magistracy of the *New-Netherlands?* How long did each remain in office? What stations or offices did they fill prior to their appointment here? Were they removed by death or resignation, or for ill behaviour? If in either of the latter ways, how were they disposed of afterwards?[53]

A number of concerned citizens responded to the Society's list of queries, which continued to be published through 1811. The originator was probably the Reverend Samuel Miller (1769–1850), who had begun assembling information on the Dutch

colony as early as 1797. Miller, one of the founders of the
Society, a distinguished and very learned Presbyterian minister,
never thought small. In *A Brief Retrospect of the Eighteenth
Century*, Miller summarized and analyzed the history, philosophy, science, and literature of an entire century only three years
after that century had closed, a prodigious intellectual
undertaking.[54] For his history of New York, he was almost as
ambitious: his papers at the New-York Historical Society include a working table of contents of 47 chapters. Although he
had obtained a surprisingly large amount of historical data, including translations of Dutch records, he outlined not a history of
New York but an elephantine guidebook to the state's history,
geography and geology, plants and animals, laws, customs, and
almost anything else one could wish to know about New York.

Irving, then, was competing historically with an official historian, and when he won, or realized he was going to win, he
laughed at the loser and those who supported him. Miller's history remained unwritten, although he continued to collect information until 1814, when he departed for Princeton. After this
date, the Society began to publish some of the information he
had received, none of which had been available to Irving, although, in a further witty gesture, he did use some of it for his
1848 revision because some of Miller's papers had been published by the Society in the 1840s. Instead, he had to rely on
what he could find in 1809; since he found so little, he thanked
the serious historians for what they had not done.

Had the Society produced anything to commemorate the bi-
centenary of Henry Hudson's discovery in 1609? Only a
party, not a history. On September 4, 1809, exactly 200 years
after the first Dutchman had touched land at Sandy Hook, New
Jersey, the Society celebrated accordingly, listening to a grave
and learned address by that acknowledged expert, the Reverend
Samuel Miller, the future historian of New York. Then everyone
went to dinner. The members of the Society thought so highly of
the oration that they waited two years to publish it.

Irving managed to slide the *History* into the Hudson bicen-

tenary of 1809, another joke at the expense of the official proclamations, addresses, and dinners. He did not choose 1809 by accident, because he had been working on the book, in some fashion or other, since some time in 1807,[55] although he does not
mention the work in his letters until the summer and fall of
1809. After the death of his fiancée Matilda Hoffman on April
26, 1809, he had gone to the home of Judge William P. Van
Ness in Kinderhook; in June he was back in the city, carrying a
manuscript; in August and September he stayed at Ravenswood,
the estate of the Hoffmans near Hellgate on the East River,
writing and revising; in November he was in Philadelphia,
where the *History* was printed.[56] It appeared, most appropriately, on December 6, the feast-day of the patron saint of
New Amsterdam, Saint Nicholas, when the ancestor of Santa
Claus distributes presents to both good and bad children.

The dedication, the year of publication, the day of publication
were, unlike Kieft or Von Poffenburgh, designed for New Yorkers
only. Irving's other bit of outside work was a prepublication and
a postpublication literary hoax. The former is well known, because when he revised the *History* for the last time in 1848, the
author reprinted the five newspaper notices which preceded publication: the announcement of Diedrich Knickerbocker's sudden
disappearance from his hotel (October 26); a report that the old
man had been spotted on the road north of Albany (November
6); the hotel owner's notice that unless Knickerbocker paid his
bill, " *a very curious kind of a written book*" found in his room
would be published to pay off the debt (November 16); a prepublication notice for the book (November 28); and an advertisement on the day of publication (December 6).[57] Since Irving
was not in New York during most of this six-week publicity
campaign, his friends could have supplied some of the notices.

Only the prepublication notices are included in the 1848 revision of *A History of New York*, but the fact is that the Knickerbocker hoax continued after December 6, 1809. When he reported what had happened to Knickerbocker after his book had
been published, in enlarging the "Account of the Author" for the

1812 revision, Irving mentioned a letter Knickerbocker had sent to the hotel owner, Seth Handaside, expressing concern at the book's appearance:

> . . . as thereby he was prevented from making several impor-
> tant corrections and alterations; as well as from profiting by
> many curious hints which he had collected during his travels
> along the shores of the Tappan Sea and his sojourn at Haver-
> straw and Esopus.[58]

Such a letter, with Seth's brief response, can be found in the *American Citizen,* January 23, 1810. It is worth reprinting in full because it has never been published since 1810:

MR. EDITOR.

As you seem to take very kind interest in the affairs of Mr. Diedrick Knickerbocker, I am happy to inform you that we have just received news of the poor old gentleman. The fol-lowing letter from him was handed to my wife the day before yesterday, by a tall country–man, who had chalked the num-ber of my house on his hat crown.

TO MR. SETH HANDASIDE.

WORTHY SIR,—It is a matter of exceeding great surprise to me when by accident I learned this morning, that after I had been for some time advertised in the newspapers as miss-ing, my history was published without receiving my last correc-tions, as also without my consent or approbation. I do not so much blame as lament this hasty measure, as the object of my mysterious absence was to collect some information of great importance to my work.

Not thinking to be absent long, I departed from your house without mentioning my intention, lest it should awaken the curiosity of your worthy spouse, who between ourselves, my honest Seth, gives herself too much trouble about the affairs of those around her—poor woman—may Heaven reward her for the same! As the weather was fine, I travelled a foot by easy stages through Manhattanville, Spikingdevil, Kingsbridge, Phillipsburgh, and so on, until I arrived at Dobb's Ferry, where I crossed over to the Slote and thence proceeded to Coeymans Patent, to the house of my esteemed friend Judge Lott, where I have been ever since entertained with true patriarchal hospitality. This worthy gentleman is come of one of the most ancient Dutch families in this country, and has in his possession the papers of his late excellent kinsman, Mr. Abraham Lott, formerly Treasurer of this Colony. From this valuable collection I have selected much interesting matter, as well as from frequent conversations with the valuable burgers of Tappan, who have given me divers wonderful particulars about the great factions of the *Blue skins* and the *Copper heads,* which anciently raged with great violence among the *Flodders,* and the *Van Schaiks,* and other potent families on the banks of the Hudson, and even occasioned not a little bitterness among the *Patricians* of Albany. But all these curious and unheard of matters which would have redounded so highly to the embellishment of my history, and the instruction of the world, with many others which it is useless to mention, your unfortunate precipitancy has buried, I fear, in eternal oblivion.

To account for my very long absence and apparent disregard of your advertisements, I must inform you; as to the first, that I have been confined by a tedious and lingering sickness, the consequence no doubt of my intense studies and incessant ponderings; and as to the second, none of your advertisements ever reached my retreat. Among the many laudable regulations instituted by the Sage Burgers of this very ancient and small town, they have banished all newspapers whatsoever, conceiving them to be mere vehicles of false politics, false morality, and false information; and moreover common disturbers of the peace of the community. Hence it is as rare a thing to see a newspaper here as a Yankee—and a politician is as uncommon a monster, as a chattering Whale or a dumb Woman. This being the case I should doubtless have still remained ignorant of the publication of my history, but for the singular accident of a newspaper being smuggled into the town under the specious pretext of serving as a wrapper to half a dozen pounds of sugar, which my friend Squire Van Loon had sent for, to Albany. The appearance of the pestilent scroll occasioned much the same sensation as would the introduction of a bale of cotton, or a bag of coffee among our old women and medical Editors, during the yellow fever. With much difficulty I obtained permission to read it, under a solemn promise to burn it, and scatter the ashes to the four winds of Heaven, the next moment. From this paper did I first learn the advertisement of my disappearance, and the subsequent publication of my history.

I regret exceedingly this last premature step, and particularly its having been published by Messrs. Inskeep and Bradford, instead of my much esteemed friend Mr. Evert Duyckingh, who is a lineal descendant from one of the ancient heroes of the Manhattoes, and whose grand father and my grand father were just like brothers. As, however, I trust that Messrs. Inskeep and Bradford, though not Dutchmen, are still very honest good sort of men, I expect they will account with me for my lawful share of the profits. In the mean time, as I am going to pass some time with my relations at Scaghtikoke, who are amazingly anxious to see me, I request that you will direct the bookseller to transmit a copy of my book, in my name, to my worthy cozen the Congressman who is now at Washington, where I have little doubt but it will be of marvellous edification to him in the discharge of his high duties. You will likewise present a copy to the City Librarian, to whose friendly attentions I was much obliged in the course of my labours, and to whom I beg you will remember me in the most cordial manner.

The book bound in vellum with brass clasps, containing the

correct records of the city, which you found in my room, you will be good enough to return, with my heartly thanks, to Mr. Peter P. Goelet and his brother Ralsey, who were so kind as to allow me the use of it. You will likewise please to call on Col. Henry Rutgers, and return him a large roll of papers ritten in Dutch, which lie on the desk in my room, giving at the same time my best acknowledgements for all his kindness, and a copy of my work neatly bound.

As to my saddle bags you may keep them with you until my cozen the Congress man returns, who will call for them and bring them to Scaghtikoke. Do not fail to send several copies up to my relations, and one to myself, for I long most vehemently to pore over my excellent little history, which I make no doubt will furnish me with abundant reading for the rest of my life.

With kind remembrances

to your worthy help mate,

I am, my honest Seth,

truly Your's,

DIEDERICK KNICKERBOCKER.

Such, Mr. Editor, is the letter I received, and I posted immediately with it to the Stuyvesant family, who have been very anxious about the old gentleman, and have made repeated enquiries after him. They were quite overjoyed to hear of his safety, and in the fullness of their hearts, declared, that the historian of their illustrious ancestor should never want. To make good their words they have provided a snug little rural retreat on their estate for him, where poor old Diederick may end his days comfortably in the neighbourhood of his favourite city, and lay his bones in peace in his beloved island of Manna hata. I have written him word of this munificient gift;

in the mean while I could not refrain from making known to the public a circumstance, which reflects such great credit on this truly worthy and respectable family.

I am sir with great respect,

your humble servant,

SETH HANDASIDE.[59]

Before this, in the same newspaper, on December 30, 1809, had appeared a long letter from Christian Brinkersnuff describing Knickerbocker's family and his education. And the *Evening Post* of December 27 had printed a short statement from Ludwick Von Bynkerfeldt testifying that he was a friend of Diedrich. Irving's mention of the January 23, 1810, letter from Knickerbocker in the second edition of the *History* indicates that he was the writer of the January 23 letter, and certainly the prose sounds like that Knickerbocker used in the *History*. As with the prepublication notices, the other two items could have been contributed by Irving's friends. In any case, the hoax did continue for another six weeks after the publication. Moreover, the two longer items appeared in a newspaper edited by James Cheetham, who had been a rabid defender of Jefferson until the middle of 1809. Irving and his friends may have honored him for his apostasy.

This long letter may properly be called the last piece of writing from the pen of the eighteenth-century Diedrich Knickerbocker, for in an addition to the 1812 edition of *A History of New York*, the author's death is recounted. The historian dies, ironically, after some of his very satisfied readers, the descendants of Peter Stuyvesant, award him a house on their lands near the East River, where the neighboring marshes give him a mortal fever. That death, another literary joke, was a real one, because the Irving of 1812 and later is a much different writer.

Behind all this literary trickery, the jibes at the collectors of history and their remembrances of things past, behind the traditional ruses of a fake author and a fake manuscript, one can see the sparkle of the literary salon, not the glow of the family fireside, the wit of the eighteenth century, not the sentiment of the Victorian age. Thus Irving ended the first part of his literary career looking backward.

In 1812, he made Knickerbocker a better storyteller. By 1848, he expressed his pleasure at seeing "Knickerbocker" used with pride by New Yorkers. But "Gotham" would have been just as appropriate for locating Knickerbocker ice and Knickerbocker bread. Worried if his revised edition would be successful because his former publisher had twice turned him away,[60] he decided to ask for a place by the fireside—and he has had his wish. Forty years before, in a society with much different ideas about the function of literature, he had written some of the best satire in all of American literature, out-historied the historians, and dazzled the town.

Sunnyside:
From Saltbox to Snuggery to Shrine

Andrew B. Myers

JUDGING FROM the number and frequency of the visitors to Washington Irving's Westchester County home, Sunnyside, during the last decades of the author's long life (1783–1859), this Hudsonside estate, and its resident squire, were widely regarded as American landmarks. All the available records clearly indicate that many of Irving's contemporaries thought of a visit, announced or unannounced, to the renowned writer at home, as a kind of obligatory and beneficial pilgrimage to a literary shrine. Though by the 1850s Sunnyside was still a rattling two-hour trip by the brand new railroad some 25 miles north from the Manhattan terminus, and at least as long a journey by road or river, for a remarkable number of the known and unknown in the Knickerbocker world of Washington Irving, the personal experience of at least a few hours at Sunnyside was a "must."

Before this small host of visitors, however, let us first get the prospective host there himself. Washington Irving returned to his native land in May 1832, after 17 years' absence in Europe. Immediately behind him was a stint of service in London as First Secretary, and even on occasion Chargé d'Affaires, at the American embassy. Before that it had been Spain, especially in Andalusia, from whence as *The Alhambra* (1832) displays, he had been stolen from this real castle in Spain by the unexpected distinction of a front-line diplomatic appointment. No need to list the honor roll of literary successes and social triumphs that had prompted the nation's leaders to capitalize on Irving's international reputation to bestow this responsible post on a now middle-aged expatriate, but these achievements reached back through years of residence and work in France also, and Germany, and the British Isles, to the publication of the best-selling *Sketch Book* in 1819–20. A decade before that, Diedrich Knickerbocker's *A History of New York* (1809) had been a dilettante's triumph; what followed was professional expertise and widespread acclaim.

Another triumph was his return in 1832 to a vastly changed Jacksonian America. His native New York, as conscious surrogate for the nation, celebrated Irving's reappearance appropriately. It was too early for the fireboat-up-the-bay salute, or the ticker tape parade up Broadway to City Hall. Nonetheless, Irving's birthplace rose to the occasion with a private tour, and more important for literary history, a public dinner at the substantial City Hotel, a formal occasion that became a yardstick by which to measure future testimonials. Hundreds of eminent guests paid homage to their literary hero who, inherent shyness notwithstanding, returned their congratulations with an unwonted burst of eloquence. On his feet, though nervous before the expectant crowd, he apostrophized the New York City that had grown so enormously since his boyhood in the presidency of the George Washington for whom he had been patriotically named:

As I sailed up our beautiful bay, with a heart swelling with old recollections and delightful associations, I was astonished to see its once wild features brightening with populous villages and noble piles, and a seeming city extending itself over heights I had left covered with green forests. [*the text here notes "The allusion probably was to Brooklyn"*] But how shall I describe my emotions when our city rose to sight, seated in the midst of its watery domain, stretching away to a vast extent; when I beheld a glorious sunshine lighting up the spires and domes, some familiar to memory, others new and unknown, and beaming upon a forest of masts of every nation, extending as far as the eye could reach? I have gazed with admiration upon many a fair city and stately harbor, but my

admiration was cold and ineffectual, for I was a stranger, and
had no property in the soil. Here, however, my heart
throbbed with pride and joy as I admired. I had a birthright
in the brilliant scene before me: "This was my own, my native
land!"[1]

Diedrich Knickerbocker, in 1809 last seen disappearing up the
Albany Post Road, had returned in the flesh. Irving closed, after
rounds of applause, with a toast, "Our City—May God continue
to prosper it."

Washington Irving could, were he less candid about the limits
of his own gifts, have taken foolish pride in all this adulation.
But natural "pride and joy" notwithstanding, he must have reflected on the poignant fact that even here also he had not yet
any real "property in the soil." In his homeland he had no home
of his own. To be certain, he did have a sort of mortgage of the
spirit on the Knickerbocker terrain he had done so much to
dramatize in letters, but as a fiftyish and lifelong bachelor, and
one long absent abroad, in truth he had no New York dwelling
of his own. He was still a wandering youngest son, long, as a
family pride, indulged by his brothers, themselves successful in
business, the law, and public life, and equally indulged by happily married sisters and their numerous children, but he had
never put a roof over his head. And for the first few years
following this open-armed welcome, given by strangers, old
friends, and his tightly knit clan, Irving, after a "See America
First" tour of the country, including the frontier West, usually
lived with his widowed brother Ebenezer at No. 3 Bridge
Street in lower Manhattan, a family gathering place affectionately called "The Hive."

In the relaxed months there, as for a brief time his pen was
put down, and he rested on fresh homegrown laurels, Irving
reacquainted himself not only with a new metropolis around
him, but also with old haunts beyond, in what this Knickerbocker generation sometimes called "rus-urban" surroundings.
At some early point in these characteristic rambles his eye was
caught, while visiting one nephew's purchase of land in the

Washington Irving
Sunnyside - June 17th 1850

"Sunnyside" by Benson Lossing (1813–1891), from his 1850 pencil sketch in the Library of Sleepy Hollow Restorations. The original is signed and dated by Washington Irving June 17, 1850.

small northward village of Tarrytown, by what he wrote of in a family letter as "that little cottage" on the adjoining Van Tassel farm. This stood about two miles south of the market town of Tarrytown, above a cove commonly identified as Wolfert's Landing. The post office, taking its name from a local land-owner, was "Dearman, N.Y." The cottage was an ordinary stone house, of colonial origins, which has subsequently been de-scribed as "merely another venerable Dutch farm cottage, with a fat central chimney" and which "looked very much like the common colonial salt box."[2] Ownership of the property can be traced back through a series of agricultural tenants to begin-nings as a minuscule part of the huge Westchester County manorial grant held by the seventeenth-century Dutch-born merchant-prince, who later englished his name as Frederick Philipse.

At this point in career Irving had finally cast his lot with his homeland, never expecting to leave it for long again. The pros-pects for the expanding United States, which were soon to jus-tify westward thrust with the imperialist slogan of Manifest Destiny, were exciting even for so cosmopolitan a person as he. And there was a sense of security (albeit temporary as events like the Panic of 1837 proved) in surveying his own pioneering victories over the uncertainties of income in his very chancy call-ing. Washington Irving seemed a fixed star in our uncrowded literary firmament, even though Edgar Allan Poe in 1838, brash in a private letter though never on this subject in print, could question, "What is due to the pioneer solely, and what to the wri-ter?"[3] Whatever his future might be a veteran Irving was now making the most of the comfortable present, and in current Knickerbocker fashion made, along with Wall Street specula-tions, another investment—this time in a home. He bought the little working farm, saltbox stone cottage, and ten acres; the div-idends this purchase would pay were to be long and happy years at Sunnyside.

On June 7, 1835, Irving finally took title to the now empty Van Tassel homestead. He was a hale 52 years of age, and at once addressed himself energetically, with all kinds of pleasant assistance in conversation from relatives, and more practical help from local workmen, to plans for turning his rather commonplace-looking, though potentially handsome, riverbank and upland holding into a gentleman's miniature estate. New York had not yet developed the luxury of professional architects, at least as our century would identify them. Instead, shared efforts of an artist interested in such matters, and an experienced master builder, plus an owner's idiosyncratic wishes, if any, produced adequate working sketches. Irving was able to enlist the skills of the young painter George Harvey, a near neighbor at Hastings, and their collaboration can to a degree be reconstructed from archival papers. Also, as Harold D. Cater explained it in *Washington Irving & Sunnyside*, the author on completion installed "a plaque embedded in the south gable where all could read, if they could read Dutch: "Gegrond Anno 1656—Verbeterd Door—Washington Irving Anno 1835— Geo. Harvey Bouwmeester." Translated, it reads: "Founded 1656— Improved by Washington Irving 1835—Geo. Harvey Masterbuilder." It may be there was in this as much a touch of fiction as of fact but the Knickerbocker echoes are clear.[4] For the rest of his life, almost a quarter century, this labor of love on Irving's part continued, as the whole place became a reflection of many of his instincts as a Romantic artist—the rural architecture, the household furnishings, and the landscaping. In the sum of its manifold details his one and only home became a virtual self-portrait.

Apparently Irving thought of the cottage first off as merely a retreat, "a nest, to which I can resort when in the mood."[5] Meantime he lived in the city, increasingly troubled by unexpected financial reverses, and writing again, as in *The Crayon Miscellany* (1835). By September of that year he had actually moved into the cottage, on the heels of retreating builders, and, willynilly, found himself making it his regular dwelling. Both house and grounds would become in a sense his wife and children. Sunnyside once occupied was not only a permanent possession he cherished, but also a frequent challenge to his creative imagination. This was no toy, to be played with and dropped.

For one thing, good years or bad, it gave him a sense of satisfaction, as evidence of the international acclaim that he had earned, although, to repeat, as a shrewd critic of his own uneven achievements, he was never prone to vanity. For another, Sunnyside, as an aesthetic change of pace offered welcome opportunities to adapt and improve according to his personal sensitivities, with only an occasional look at current fashions. At times he worked at the property as hard as ever he had under the spur of his muses, and in the end became in both literature, and life, a tastemaker. As Joseph Butler, Curator of Sleepy Hollow Restorations, has put it, "In the final analysis, it is the highly personal taste of Washington Irving that is sensed in every part of the property."[6]

On November 24, 1835, he could write to brother Peter in France, long his companion in European travels, "Like all meddlings with stone and mortar, the plan has extended as I built, until it has ended in a complete, though moderate-sized family residence." These meddlings included not only stone and mortar but iron, at least in the sense that Irving, after the offer of an ironwork gift for his new house from Knickerbocker magnate Gouverneur Kemble, to be made in his own foundry upriver at Cold Spring, was delighted to suggest details. In a letter of November 14, 1836, he wrote that Kemble, "who was at my cottage a few days since, offered to furnish me with two gothic (sic) seats of cast iron, and to have them cast in the highlands, if I would send him patterns." Irving did so posthaste and in due course two iron benches were delivered, approximating his submitted sketches. These "gothic" seats, long familiar items in pictures of the entrance to Sunnyside, still stand on either side of the door opening to the front of the house.[7]

Once he was settled in, Irving's hospitality at this "Roost," as first he called it, was quickly tested, and beyond the predictable circle of blood relations and lifelong intimates. It is probable his first outside visitor was the immigrant financeer John Jacob Astor, a more recent friend, at whose behest the author had undertaken his first farwestern history, *Astoria* (1836). The volume was just going through the press as he was settling into Sunnyside. To Pierre Munro Irving, a favorite nephew destined to be his uncle's literary executor and official biographer, Washington would write, on December 12, 1835, "Old Astor most unexpectedly paid me a visit at the cottage about a month since. . . . He landed at Tarrytown, and hired a vehicle, which brought him to the cottage door. He spent two days here, and promised to repeat his visit as soon as there shall be good sleighing."[8] John Jacob Astor taken for a sleigh ride?

During the winter of 1836–37 Irving completed his second Rocky Mountains fur-trade volume, *The Adventures of Captain Bonneville* (1837), the first manuscript completed at the country retreat, whose study was now his permanent workshop. The spring that followed Irving received his first foreign visitor of eminence, Charles Louis Napoleon Bonaparte, young head of the surviving dynasty, later to be Napoleon III. His arrival is a token of the American writer's continental reputation. Pierre writes:

> Among the memorable events of this season at the cottage, was a visit from the present Emperor of France, then simple Louis Napoleon, who after having been a prisoner of state for some months on board of a French man-of-war, was set at liberty on our shores at Norfolk, early in the spring of 1837. From Norfolk he came immediately to New York, where he remained about two months, and then returned to Europe. It was during this interval that he made his visit to the "Roost," accompanied by a young French count, and escorted by a neighbor, Mr. Anthony Constant, with whom he had been passing a day or two, and who previously announced to Mr. Irving his intention of bringing him to breakfast. Mr. Irving enjoyed the visit, and was much interested in the peculiar position of his somewhat quiet guest, though little anticipating the dazzling career which awaited him.[9]

A year later, with Irving by now very much a fixture on the downtown Knickerbocker scene, even if a commuter to Manhattan, he was visited by a more native type of political figure, in fact a committee with nomination for office aforethought. In the spring of 1838 another family missive by the ruler of the "Roost" explained, "Yesterday I had a full deputation from Tammany Hall at the cottage, informing me I had been unanimously and vociferously nominated as Mayor, and hoping I would consent to be a candidate. Of course I declined."[10] Whatever the unaggressive Irving was spared, it may well be the city lost a chance for a new *History*, of extraordinary comic possibilities.

Speaking of the mayoralty, Knickerbocker businessman and civic leader Philip Hone, the Mayor in 1825, visited Sunnyside in the late summer of 1839, on a leisurely trip up the Hudson with his wife. His remarkable diary reads in part, on September 18, as reported by historian Allan Nevins:

"Our friend Geoffrey Crayon's cottage appeared rather to a disadvantage after leaving its tasteful and elegant neighbor a mile or two further up," he writes. "It is a quaint, Dutch-looking cabin, with small rooms, inconvenient and only one story high; but the admirers of the gentle Geoffrey think, no doubt, that one *story* of his is worth more than a dozen of other people's."[11]

These varied distractions aside, during 1839 Irving did in fact use his pleasant surroundings for a brief essay or two, sent down to the *Knickerbocker,* a leading monthly literary magazine whose principal editor, Lewis Gaylord Clark, would become a familiar figure at the cottage. In a "Letter To The Editor" in March of that year, promising regular contributions, Irving, admittedly overjoyed as the "possessor of the Roost!," potboiling motive notwithstanding, wove a web of fancy uniting the present with a local past that included a veritable Diedrich Knickerbocker—"it is from his elbow-chair, and his identical old Dutch writing-desk, that I pen this rambling epistle." For the May issue he contributed "Sleepy Hollow, By Geoffrey Crayon, Gent.," musings that made up a mere filler, unashamedly shining in the light of the *Sketch Book's* reflected glory. He fantasized, again with Diedrich as elbow companion, about "boyish" wan-

derings in the nearby hills and valleys, and fishing in the Pocan-
tico. Closing, he brought the real Sleepy Hollow up to date,
with "the sad conviction" that he and it were witnessing "the
last lingerings of the good old Dutch times in this favored region."[12] This, aside from being good copy for readers attuned to
Romantic longings, represented an ingrained regret in Irving at
the destruction always wrought by time. This lifelong tendency
explains in part the determination with which he added antiquarian touches to his new-old domain.

To ring the changes year by year on all the guests at Sunnyside—for so he had dubbed it by 1841—is not necessary in this
rapid survey. But it should be noted that some likely invitees, as
far as we can discover never came at all, and thereby hangs a
modest tale or two. In the late 1830s he was close enough to the
President of the United States, New York's own Martin Van
Buren, to be offered in 1838, and by conditioned reflex to decline, the cabinet post of Secretary of the Navy. Not for him a
troublesome public post, which went then to Irving's old shield-
mate in early Knickerbocker literary wars, James Kirke Paulding,
a Hyde Park gentleman farmer, whose own presence at Sunnyside needs to be better documented. As for Van Buren, he was invited several times during his White House years, on one occasion,
July 2, 1839, with this teasing bait, "I can only promise you plain
country fare, but you shall have chickens stuffed in the true
Dutch style as we used to have them doing our tours through
the Dutch neighborhoods of the Hudson." This culinary temp-
tation notwithstanding we cannot be certain he appeared. In
any event, political, not necessarily personal differences, tended
to separate the two men after Van Buren lost the election of
1840. Though it is certain these two prominent New Yorkers met
elsewhere over the years, apparently during his long forced retirement the Red Fox of Kinderhook never journeyed to see Irving in Tarrytown.[13]

The most lionized European visitor to these United States
since Lafayette in 1824 was the hugely popular Charles Dickens,
whose tour of the country in 1842 was some times a canoniza-
tion in life and at others a circus. He wrote Irving beforehand

most admiringly, including this praise, "Diedrich Knickerbocker I have worn to death in my pocket, and yet I should show you his mutilated carcass with a joy past all expression." When Dickens arrived the two favorites inevitably were brought together in public. Indeed it was Irving, much flustered as always on a dais, who was called upon to give the toast to Dickens at a festive dinner in New York. But Dickens the consummate artist and Dickens the ebullient man were not enough alike to entirely please the soft-spoken and fastidious American. Some ink has been spilled on a private coolness in the latter that purportedly developed, but, the uncertainties of this aside, the fact remains that, too rushed, or uninvited, Dickens never made his way to Sunnyside.[14] The forthcoming volumes of Irving correspondence may throw more light on this loss to literary history.

By 1842 Washington Irving was rounding out five years and more of happy life at Sunnyside, joined for good now by his retired older brother Ebenezer and often by nephews and nieces galore. One very favorite niece, Sarah Sanders Paris, had already been married at the cottage, on March 31, 1841, to Thomas Wentworth Storrow, Jr., son of an old friend of her uncle's in Europe.[15] Unhappily, this nuptial chapter in the Sunnyside story had been preceded by a sadder one, when on June 27, 1838, Peter Irving, *quondam* physician, early Knickerbocker editor and writer, and Washington's constant companion overseas, died at Sunnyside.

Such personal intensities notwithstanding, more prosaic comings and goings developed, as for example the appearance in 1842 of the now forgotten writer Van Bibber, whom Pierre calls, "an early literary pilgrim to Sunnyside."[16] He can stand for a developing traffic of lesser Knickerbocker luminaries who were persistent about paying respectful court. And at the same time the master of the house was attracting this attention the house itself, and the grounds, which had been increased to its final size of 24 acres, were doing almost as well. Andrew Jackson Downing, a young New Yorker already influential as an early landscape architect, was making a deep impression by successfully adapting the so-called "natural" English landscape style, aristocratic in its origins, to the practical needs and democratic vanities of his American countrymen of lesser means. His lengthy illustrated text, *The Theory And Practise Of Landscape Gardening* (1841), regularly reprinted, became a classic in its own time. In it Sunnyside is described, and with an engraving to illustrate, as one good example of our "Rural Architecture" of interest as "partaking somewhat of the English cottage mode, but retaining strongly marked symptoms of its Dutch origin." Downing also praised the cottage, or "villa" as he wrote in a private letter then, by noting, "There is scarcely a building or place more replete with interest in America, than the cottage of Washington Irving near Tarrytown."[17]

For all Irving knew, life had settled into a finished pattern, and as a respected and senatorial figure in our boisterous young congress of the arts, he was content. Quite abruptly this pleasant pattern was broken. In February 1842, without notice, President John Tyler, at the urging of Secretary of State Daniel Webster, chose Irving to serve as our Minister in Madrid. Considering our amateur tradition of a *corps diplomatique,* and also Irving's knowledge of Spain, this was a logical choice, and, as it proved, one enthusiastically received, both here and in Europe. The nominee, astonished at first, after reflection, accepted, conscious of a debt he felt he owed to a nation that had long cherished and rewarded him. But the duty took him overseas again, and as it turned out, for four years, a long time at his age. Nevertheless, as family correspondence shows, Sunnyside, and all it had come to mean, was never far from his thoughts. Just one special dream of home and fireside needs to be mentioned, and that to suggest the openly sentimental legendry that was growing up about the place and its people. Irving had more influence than is commonly realized on the evolution of Christmas customs in North America, particularly because of the continuing success of the Old Christmas pieces in *The Sketch Book.* Listen to the Envoy Extraordinary and Minister Plenipotentiary writing home to his niece Sarah Irving on January 13, 1843:

I thought of you all at dear little Sunnyside on Christmas day, and heartily wished myself there to eat my Christmas dinner among you. I hope you kept up Christmas in the usual style, and that the cottage was decked with evergreens. You must not let my absence cause any relaxations in the old rules and customs of the cottage; everything must go on the same as it did when I was there.[18]

Irving served until 1846 and then, at the age of 62, resigned at the next change of administration. He reached Sunnyside at last on September 19, 1846, thrice ready to drop the formal title "His Excellency, Mr. Irving."

In the spring of 1847, following Irving's return from Spain, the distinguished historian William Hickling Prescott, author of *Ferdinand and Isabella* and *Conquest of Mexico,* visited his New York publisher to discuss his current work, *Conquest of Peru.* Having made the trip from New England, he did not want to miss the opportunity of talking shop about Spain with the recently returned former Minister. Prescott described his visit at Sunnyside with Irving in a letter to George Sumner: "He is in pretty good health, and watches with parental satisfaction over a numerous family of feathered bipeds, who seem to constitute at once his plague and his pleasure."[19] Apparently Henry Brevoort was also at Sunnyside on that April day, for in a letter to Irving on January 3, 1856, Prescott would write, concerning some correspondence he had received from him: "Its date from Sunnyside reminds me of the pleasant day I passed in company with your early friend Brevoort, and mine of later years." Brevoort's visits have so far been difficult to document, even though Brevoort was a lifelong intimate, beginning with fancy-free days and nights on the town, happily shared with Irving as one of the Knickerbocker "Lads of Kilkenny."[20]

As soon as Irving returned to Sunnyside, with hardly a refreshing pause, the itch to improve and reconstruct began, with physical results that produced the image most widely recognized throughout the country at and after midcentury, via the work of industrious engravers, lithographers, painters and, finally, photographers, all of whom produced likenesses or impressions either in book and magazine illustrations, or in separate canvases or multiple prints. In particular, the cottage, seen from one perspective or another, caught the eye of a number of the Hudson River school of artists, for one thing because of its proximity to the "Rhine" of America, for another the quiet charm of its relatively unspoiled rustic qualities. After Irving's death, one rather artificial view of Sunnyside achieved the distinction, in popular graphics, of circulation as a Currier and Ives print.

The resettled squire on September 18, 1847, could write back to Madrid, to Sabina, Mrs. Henry O'Shea, the young Spanish wife of a banker friend there:

> I found my place very much out of order, my house in need of additions and repairs and the whole establishment in want of completion. I set to work immediately, and kept on at all times and seasons, in defiance of heat and cold, wind and weather and as I was pretty much my own architect; projector and landscape gardener, and had but rough hands to work under me, I have been kept busy out of doors from morning until night and from months end to months end until within a week or two past, when I brought my labors to a close, or rather relinquished them, finding I had spent all the money in my pocket and fagged myself into an irritation of the system which has rendered me almost as lame as I used to be in Madrid. I have now returned to my books and my study, and taken up my long neglected pen; and hope once more to go on according to my old habitudes.[21]

His interior redesigning, which primarily enlarged accommodations and services for guests and live-in help, for the first time took him upstairs to the privacy of a separate bedroom of his own. Hitherto the downstairs study, mentioned above, served for both rest and for literary work, especially since it housed the best of his library. The most unusual new construction, however, was an exterior innovation, a solid tower of three stories, at the back of the house, topped by a slanted roof supporting a tiny cupola—sans bell. Gouverneur Kemble, seeing it while passing on a riverboat, teased Irving into this response to his old friend of *Salmagundi* days:

> As to the *pagoda* about which you speak, it is one of the most useful additions that ever was made to a house, besides being so ornamental. It gives me laundry, store rooms, pantries, servants' rooms, coal cellar, &, &, &, converting what was once a rather make-shift little mansion into one of the most complete snuggeries in the country, as you will confess when you come to see and inspect it.[22]

From saltbox to snuggery! On to shrine.

This transition was materially assisted by Irving's taking up again that "long neglected pen." The need for secure income was pressing, at least if he was to keep up a comfortable style of living, not just as a gentleman farmer himself, but unselfishly, for others in his household as well. Ebenezer's two spinster daughters, Catherine and Sarah, would, as "The Misses Irving" their calling cards announced, be the chatelaines at Sunnyside for decades after his passing, a decade hence.[23] On July 26, 1848, Irving signed with a new publisher, George P. Putnam of Manhattan, an entrepreneur thoroughly respectable but not with great resources, to try together an experiment in American publishing, a multivolumed Author's Revised Edition, the first of its kind. Much of Irving's key effort would be made in the small study at Sunnyside, with friend Putnam a frequent visitor.[24]

To shorten the story of the next half dozen years, this Author's Revised Edition (1848–51), in 15 volumes, was a success. It not only made money for both in the literary marketplace, but introduced Irving to a whole new generation of mid-Victorian readers. After all, it was almost 50 years since first he had broken into print, and the "Geoffrey Crayon" alter ego of *The Sketch Book*, and other title pages, was decades behind him. At the speed at which New York and the nation were growing, for many he must have seemed beforehand just a museum piece. For others he had remained an old familiar face gladly recog-

nized in a crowd of pushy newcomers. In any event, in a republic lacking a long and glorious history, and eagerly searching for
heroes, the lucky combination of Irving's pen and his personality
now finally turned him (how rightly or wrongly is perhaps a
scholars' quarrel) into a national institution. And he carried Sunnyside along with him. The comments of Knickerbocker essayist
and poetaster Nathaniel Parker Willis in the *Home Journal* for
November 3, 1849, reflect mixed aspects of the apotheosis gradually taking place, "We are glad to see that honors and successes
accumulate upon our gifted countryman. A beautiful public
square and a large popular hotel bear his name; and a new line
of stages is to be adorned with the same classic appellative." By
contrast, when in the same year Edgar Allan Poe died tragically,
and only at 40, he was, except by a faithful few, "unwept, unhon-
ored, and unsung."

By the end of the 1840s and into the 1850s Romanticism was
reaching its apogee in the finest prose and verse of the American
Renaissance, as it came to be known. As we see it now, this was
a full flowering of native genius, in the work of major artists like
Emerson, Hawthorne, and Thoreau of New England, and Melville and Whitman of New York. This coming of age artistically,
Lewis Mumford in our time aptly termed "The Golden Day."
Irving quietly basked in his allotted share of such noontime sun-
light, and not just as a tolerated grand-old-man in retirement.
The Putnam edition had blown the dust from old favorites, and
reminded younger contemporaries of the sunrise that had had to
come first. And throughout this amazing decade Irving's valetudinarian struggles with a solidly based if too often uninspired
Life of Washington, published in five volumes during 1855–59,
put his name on brand new title pages. In the progress of these
final years Sunnyside imperceptively but positively evolved
from country seat to literary shrine. Reflective of this is the oil
painting completed by Christian Schussele in 1863 "Washington
Irving and His Literary Friends at Sunnyside."[25] Much reproduced, this large canvas, using the conventions of the age, de-
picted a noble but imaginary gathering of authorial knights. Of

course, the meeting never took place, but grouped as they are around Irving, and in just that setting, these Olympians without lifting a hand helped christen a Knickerbocker Olympus.

For evidence of this a sampling of visitors must suffice, since year by year now scores of arrivals and departures punctuated simpler household affairs. And though Irving traveled away at times too, on historical investigations, or to friends or relatives in nearby states, or for example to Saratoga, as that watering place grew fashionable, the recoverable data on guests he was hospitable to at home, callers expected or unexpected, gives ample proof of a steady stream of latter-day-pilgrims who appeared, even as Irving himself had beaten his path long ago to Scott's door at Abbotsford.

In the fall of 1849 one such voyager, and from foreign shores, was the Swedish feminist and writer Fredericka Bremer, who already knew Irving's *Sketch Book* in translation. Having met Irving at a dinner party at the Hamiltons near Newburgh, she was invited to come next day to Sunnyside. It may be Irving was attracted by the persistence of a lady of letters who even intrigued, on first meeting, to have his attention distracted while she sketched him. In any case, her report to a sister at home, in a letter from Brooklyn, November 5, 1849, reads in part:

> His home or villa, which stands on the banks of the Hudson, resembles a peaceful idyll; thick masses of ivy clothe one portion of the white walls and garland the eaves. Fat cows gaze in a meadow right before the window. Within, the room seemed full of summer warmth and peace, and gave the appearance of something living. One felt that a cordial spirit, full of the best sentiments of the soul, lived and worked there.

She continued with compliments to Irving's healthy appearance at this age, and noticed that he was "at this time occupied with his *Life of Mahomet* which will shortly be sent to press."[26]

Two visitors in the summer of 1850 had differing motives for the trip which one, at least, took on the Hudson River Railroad that had been operating for the past year, after the tracks had shorn Sunnyside of its watery western margin. In June the active historiographer Benson J. Lossing, on a tour of inspection for his two-volume *The Pictorial Field-Book of The Revolution* (to be published in 1852 with hundreds of wood engravings from his own sketches) appeared and prepared himself the better for a text that would describe patriot Jacob Van Tassel's dwelling as during the war a sort of local guerrilla headquarters which the British in reprisal "sacked, plundered, and burned." Since he could no longer depict the little farmhouse rebuilt on the ruins, Lossing offered instead "Sunnyside, The Residence of Washington Irving," its successor. Sleepy Hollow Restorations has on loan from Lossing's daughter Helen, Mrs. F. E. Johnson, the original pencil sketch, which Irving inscribed "Washington Irving Sunnyside—June 17th 1850." Mrs. Johnson wrote on the back a close approximation of the reference to this experience, to be found in Lossing's printed text:

> This sketch was made by my father for his Field Book of the Revolution—In writing of this visit to Mr. Irving he said; "I visited Sunnyside and made the sketch. * * * It was in leafy June, and a lovelier day never smiled on the Hudson and its green bank. * * * As I sat beneath a spreading cedar sketching the unique villa, and scolded without stint by a querulous matronly cat-bird on one side, and a vixen jenny on the other, I observed Mr. Irving leading a little fair-haired grand-nephew to the river bank in search of daisies and butter cups.[27]

This basically professional visit was followed shortly by a more personal one. In July 1850 arrived the well-known, traveling English novelist, G. P. R. James. He came by early train, with his wife and three teenage children, and the day went swimmingly.[28]

The literary journalist Henry T. Tuckerman was entertained during 1851, and then published an adulatory account in Putnam's parlor table *Homes of American Authors* (1853).[29] In February 1852, as Pierre reports, "he had a visit from Clark of the *Knickerbocker*, and Leutze, the painter, who came by appointment and dined with him."[30] That same February, on the

24th in New York City, Irving joined with authors like Bryant, public men like Daniel Webster, and many other admirers in paying memorial tribute to James Fenimore Cooper, who had died at Cooperstown the previous September. Here was another notable who never came to Sunnyside though Irving would have welcomed him. Cooper was a fiercely independent spirit who managed to alienate a considerable number of contemporaries, with his strictures on American society. He also was bitter about Irving's sustained popularity, which the brilliant creator of "The Leatherstocking Tales" considered excessive. Irving's several friendly overtures had met with a gentlemanly response, but Cooper never chose to accept the offer of friendship. Thus Sunnyside never saw him.[31]

In the autumn of 1852 Irving had the company of Donald G. Mitchell ("Ike Marvel"), one of an honor guard of Irvingesque stylists now making a name in later Knickerbocker literature. Three decades afterwards, in 1883, now himself an old-timer, Mitchell recalled this visit, at the one hundredth anniversary celebration, at Tarrytown, of Irving's birth. As Irving had done for him years before, Mitchell took his listeners on a tour of the whole historic area—where the real André was captured, and the fictitious Ichabod Crane escaped—with Irving as guide, doing the driving and making his points with a "sweep of his whip-hand."[32]

Scattered across these middle years of the 1850s were visits Irving exchanged with a slightly younger Maryland friend, the minor novelist and Washington, D. C. personage, John Pendleton Kennedy, who in 1835 had dedicated his *Horse-Shoe Robinson* to Irving. Kennedy came to stay at Sunnyside in the late summer of 1853. His portrait, and that of his pretty wife Elizabeth, hang today as they did in Irving's time in the dining room where both were affectionately entertained. Willis, who accompanied Kennedy to Irving's home again in 1859, would remark, "We had two 'Mr. Kennedy's' in the dining room . . . our friend's portrait as he sat at the dining-table, hanging directly over his head."[33]

By this time in Irving's last career-within-careers he was ab-

sorbed in researches for the long germinating biography of
George Washington which would be his farewell work. Not in-
frequently these labors took the deeply commited author far
from home. Stanley T. Williams, whose exhaustive biography of
Irving in 1935 was a milestone in scholarship on the man and
the artist, wrote:

> By 1853 his correspondence on his formidable subject was vo-
> luminous, his visits to libraries incessant, and his study inten-
> sive. His business in New York suffered regular interruptions,
> and even his holidays, periods of "literary abstinence," as he
> called them, became pilgrimages to scenes identified with
> Washington. Thus at Saratoga he reconstructed the setting of
> Burgoyne's surrender. On his journeys south his new note-
> books were ever at his side; at Baltimore he scoured newspa-
> pers, and at Washington he thumbed government records and
> military dispatches. At Mount Vernon he studied the rooms,
> the furniture, and the gardens, and on February 4, 1853, he
> postponed his return to Sunnyside because of a "world of doc-
> uments to examine."[34]

In 1854, unbeknown to its first citizen, Dearman, N.Y., peti-
tioned the Postmaster General to change its name to Irvington.
The eponymous Irving had to live with the successful result and
characteristically did so without parade; but his being on the
map, in a literal sense, undoubtedly increased the number of
curiosity-seekers and well-wishers who beat various paths to Sunnyside. One well-wisher who was made welcome was the inde-
fatigable traveler and author Bayard Taylor, who would write a
friend on September 20, "I have just returned from Tarrytown,
where I spent the afternoon with Washington Irving, who is a
charming old man and a good friend of mine."[35] As for the others, in April 1855, an unsigned article in the *New-York Quarterly* stated, however accurately, "So averse is he, indeed, to ob-
servation, that he feels it to be an annoyance that troops of in-
quisitive visitors, from Tarrytown, should make Sunny-Side an
object of daily curiosity."[36] If indeed annoyed, Irving could val-

idly plead, at 72 and fighting his *Washington* into galley proof,
the need for undisturbed concentration on reading and writing.

But by all odds, the prize visitor of this year must have been
the English novelist William Makepeace Thackeray, newly arrived from home, and at the height of his fame making a second tour of the United States. In November Thackeray, while
nearby in Yonkers for a public appearance, snatched time from
a heavy schedule of lectures and receptions, to accept his
friend's invitation to call. In a letter to his teenage daughters
Anne and Harriet in Paris their father wrote, December 3-4,
1855, of his sojourn at Sunnyside.

> . . . where good old Washington Irving lives with 2 nieces
> who tend him most affectionately in a funny little in and out
> cottage surrounded by a little domain of lawns not so smooth
> as our's and woods rather small & scrubby—in little bits of
> small parlors where we were served with cake and wine—
> with a little study not much bigger than my back room, with
> old dogs trotting about the premises with fleets of ducks sail-
> ing on the ponds—a very pleasant patriarchal life.

Another letter, on December 14, to his friend Mrs. B. W.
Proctor, had this hurried remembrance, "About two hours of
quiet I have had here, whilst I went to see dear old Washington
Irving at his college [sic] on the Hudson—such a homely little
cottage with two kind little nieces to take care of the old man."[37]
One doubts Irving would have appreciated the geriatric
touches! Thackeray was more eloquent in print, after Irving's
death, when in 1860 in a "Nil Nisi Bonum" essay in London's
Cornhill magazine he turned the neat phrase, much repeated
since, that Irving "was the first ambassador whom the New
World of Letters sent to the old."

A fuller account of this hands-across-the-sea visit is preserved
in the diary of Thackeray's host in Yonkers, Frederick S. Cozzens, who wrote, in part:

> The day inexpressibly balmy and beautiful. As we rode by the
> Hudson, Thackeray kept exclaiming, "This is very jolly!"

"How jolly!" as view after view appeared. Irving was in fine spirits. Thackeray said, looking around the room, "I must take an inventory or note of the furniture, etc., so that when I write my book on America I shall be able to put all this in." "Oh," said Irving, catching the joke, "you must not forget my nieces,"—introducing them again, with mock courtesy. "This is the one that writes for me: all my stories are from her pen. This young lady is the poet of the family. She has a collection of sonnets that will astonish the world by and by. Another niece of mine is upstairs. She is the musician and painter,—a great genius, only she has never come out. I suppose I must show you my curiosities. These Moorish coins? I was riding through a field in Granada when they were ploughed up. Gave a trifle for them. The poor fellow that found them preferred current money. This fringe is from the sword-hilt of poor Boabdil. Here is a pair of spectacles that belonged to General Washington, and here is another pair that belonged to John Jacob Astor. I thought with Washington's and Astor's spectacles I might be able to see my way pretty clearly through the world."

In the conversation Thackeray said, "Willis asked me why I did not take notes of my visit. I was about to answer what I thought of such a liberty, when I remembered that he had done such things himself, and was silent." . . . "This little anchor was presented to me by some officer of the navy. It was made of the staple in the wall to which Columbus was chained."

When we rode down to Yonkers, Irving was to drive with us. He asked me to go home by the saw-mill river road. We did so. He was delighted to see this familiar ground,—had not seen it for many years . . .[38]

Not all candidates for Irving's sociable welcome fared quite so well over these same months. As a last entry for 1855 consider the note sent down to "General" George P. Morris in the city, on September 6, trying to match schedules so that this Knickerbocker friend, and founder of the literary *New-York Mirror*

(1823–42), could come up and bring a companion too. Irving had to add a postscript, "I am sorry to say I cannot offer Mr. Richards a bed as my "Spare room" is bespoke by successive visitors for some time to come. My little mansion has generally what is called a *Scotch housefull,* that is to say, rather more than it will hold."[39]

In turn 1856 had its plethora of pilgrims. For one, in the summer, Benjamin Silliman, Professor of Chemistry at Yale, and already celebrated as an outstanding American scientist, while on a Westchester jaunt paid a short visit, reported in his diary for August 20 as follows:

> This distinguished gentleman, one of the brightest stars of our literary hemisphere, came from his home, a mile from this place, and passed a long evening with us; and we had half an hour or more with him, as I have mentioned *[entry for August 19th]* at his own house. In person he is not tall; probably he may be five feet six or seven inches high; his form rather round and full, but not corpulent; his countenance florid and slightly bronzed; his lips thick; his eyes blue or gray; his expression mild and benignant, with a slight tinge of mirthfulness; his air modest, with even a shade of diffidence; his voice is not clear; but rather husky, as if catarrhal; his conversation is animated and engaging, and he appears quite as willing to hear as to speak. Having had some correspondence with him regarding his "Life of Washington," we were naturally drawn nearer together on that account; and he conversed with freedom and ease respecting his work.[40]

To round out this year, there is unassailable evidence of the presence during 1856 of the pioneering photographer F. Langenheim, since his picture of that date, of Irving seated in the porch before his front door, survives as a stereoscopic slide.[41]

To move on to 1857, during this summer N. P. Willis put in an appearance, with the result foreordained to appear in his *Home Journal,* still another in a growing number of genuflections before the altar, albeit a side altar, of Irving-and-Sunnyside.

Subtracting its Victorian sentimentalities, value remains in such biographical and autobiographical elements as these:

> Our conversation, for the half hour that we sat in that little library, turned first upon the habits of literary labor. Mr. Irving, in reply to my inquiry (whether, like Rip Van Winkle, he had "arrived at that happy age when a man can be idle with impunity"), said, "no"—that he had sometimes worked even fourteen hours a day, but that he usually sits in his study, occupied, from breakfast till dinner (both of us agreeing, that, in literary vegetation the "do" is on in the morning); and that he should be sorry to have much more leisure. He thought, indeed, that he should "die in harness."[42]

During 1858, with health because of "asthma" by now a growing worry, Irving struggled toward the conclusion of *Washington,* as dutiful at Putnam's gift desk in the study as at a monthly odyssey to Manhattan, to attend, as a civic duty, stated meetings of the Board of Trustees of the new, and free Astor Library, of which he was first President. This single instance must suffice to cover other similar obligations, impressive in both kind and number, to which Irving donated time and energy, as possible, to the very end.[43]

Meanwhile, back at Sunnyside, there were the usual interruptions. The indispensable Pierre again notes, "*April 17th, 1858.—* A Mr. T——, from the centre of Ohio, called at the cottage, as he stated, "simply to see Washington Irving before his return." He brought a letter from Horace Greeley, saying that he was no author, and only curious to have a look at him. Made a short visit, and proved to be a very good fellow."[44] Having paid ungrudgingly this price to fame and fortune, Irving must have been happier by far when in December he was visited, unheralded by card or correspondence, by Dr. Oliver Wendell Holmes, who was in the neighborhood. This Boston physician had already contributed to the sum of the Renaissance the Yankee wit and wisdom of *The Autocrat of the Breakfast Table* (1858), which delighted Irving. In reminiscences in 1860 Holmes would recall:

I learned, however, on arriving at New York, that he had been very ill of late, and that it was doubtful whether he would be in a condition to see me. At least, however, I might look upon that home of his, next to Mount Vernon, the best known and most cherished of all the dwellings in our land.

Sunnyside was *Snowyside* on that December morning; yet the thin white veil could not conceal the features of a place long familiar to me through the aid of engravings and photographs, and as stereotyped in the miraculous solid sun-pictures. The sharp-pinnacled roof, surmounted by the old Dutch weather-cock; the vine-clad cottage, with its three-arched open porch,— open on all sides, like the master's heart,—were there as I knew them, just as thousands know them who have never trodden or floated between the banks of the Hudson.

As for the ailing master of this famous house, in fact he did gird himself to appear, and the Yankee pundit had the self-limiting "half-hour's talk" with him so many others had before him. A doctor's trained eye was busy all the while, and Holmes continued, ". . . it was painful to see the labor it cost Mr. Irving to talk; and I could not forget, that, however warm my welcome, I was calling upon an invalid, and that my visit must be short. Something authorized me to allude to his illness, and my old professional instincts led me to suggest to him the use of certain palliatives which I had known to be used in some cases having symptoms which resembled his own."[45]

Washington Irving was 76 on April 3, 1859, the final year of his long and eventful life. For much of the time thereafter, Pierre Munro Irving stayed constantly beside his failing uncle, who was troubled by chronic shortness of breath and by chest pains, which may have been the asthma the family spoke of, or in more modern parlance, congestive heart failure. The *Washington* was finished by early spring too, and life became a fight for restful sleep.

All the same, and understandably, numerous old friends and associates came and went, as did beloved family, each one sensing Washington Irving's tenuous hold on life. Also, as had by

now become a habit, thoughtless or otherwise, complete strangers continued to come as well. Long accustomed to nuisances
like letters begging a lock of hair or a signature or a few lines in
his hand, the aging author was surprisingly courteous about interruptions by nameless devotees who suddenly materialized at
his much-publicized portals. It would appear that he had determined to accept these sometimes dubious honors not with angry
outrage, or glacial refusal, but in the same democratic manner
in which most of them were offered. He reserved expressions of
annoyance for private conversation. Could an institution incar-
nate, in this America, do less?[46] In any event consider this story,
by the indispensable Pierre, of one awkward visitation on the
morning of July 7, 1859:

> Just before sitting down to breakfast, a stranger called at the
> door, wishing to see Mr. Irving. The servant informed him he
> was ill—but he had come from a great distance, and begged
> to see him, if but for a few moments. Mr. Irving, excessively
> troubled at the time by shortness of breath, requested me to
> see him. I went to the door, and found a very ordinary-
> looking personage with a carpet bag. He asked if I was Mr.
> Irving. Not Mr. Washington Irving, I told him. He is ill, and
> unable to see any one. "It would be a great gratification to see
> him, if but for a few moments. Had come a great distance.
> Had called four years before, but he was not at home.
> Trusted he might not be disappointed." I returned to Mr. Irv-
> ing, and reported what he said. He went to the door and in-
> vited him into the library. The stranger took a chair, and was
> going in for a long talk, when Mr. Irving had to excuse him-
> self, from his difficulty of breathing. The stranger than asked
> for his autograph. Mr. Irving informed him he was too dis-
> tressed to write it then, but would send it to his address,
> which the stranger gave, and asked Mr. Irving his charge, say-
> ing, "It is a principle with me always to pay for such things."
> "It is a principle with me," replied Mr. Irving sharply, "never
> to take pay."

The devoted biographer added simply, "He came back quite

disgusted."⁴⁷ Fair enough, one can say for the ignorance involved, but unmistakably it was the overall good intention that
concerned Irving when wearily he went to the door.

The last visitor who need be mentioned is Knickerbocker litterateur Theodore Tilton, an editor of the *Independent*, who arrived as prearranged on November 5. The resulting interview
was printed on November 24, 1859, four days before Irving's
mercifully quick death, in his upstairs bedroom at Sunnyside.
Tilton, in a wording that had by now become almost epidemic,
called his piece "Half An Hour At Sunnyside." His account is
symbolic of the unflagging interest in the old man, and in his
storied home. In part the story ran:

> The mansion of Sunnyside has been standing for twenty-three
> years: but when first its sharp-angled roof wedged its way up
> among the branches of the old woods, the region was far
> more a solitude than now; for at that time our busy author
> had secluded himself from almost everyone but one near
> neighbor; while he has since unwittingly gathered around him
> a little community of New York merchants, whose elegant
> country-seats, opening into each other by mutual intertwining
> roads, form what looks like one vast and free estate, called on
> the timetables of the railroad by the honorary name of Ir
> vington. But even within the growing circle of his many
> neighbors, the genial old Knickerbocker still lives in true re
> tirement, entertaining his guests within echo distance of Sleepy
> Hollow—without thought, and almost without knowledge,
>
> "—how the great world
> Is praising him far off."⁴⁸

This last is smooth stuff, if a little silly as well, for the "great
world," if measured by the paths beaten to Sunnyside, was
never "far off" for long. And it reappeared within the month as
literally thousands, both high and low, journeyed hither to see
Washington Irving laid to rest, with rites that began with a cortege from Sunnyside, moved to Episcopal services at Christ

Church, Tarrytown, where he had been a communicant, and ended at the family plot in Sleepy Hollow Cemetery nearby. The frequently astringent lawyer George Templeton Strong, of another Knickerbocker generation, perhaps summed up this life best when he wrote in his diary, "He leaves a fragrant memory, personal and literary."[49]

Thereafter, Sunnyside lost much of its prominence. Neither Knickerbocker literati nor foreign dignitaries had the same reasons for making the trip to Westchester, and the casual sightseer soon found other targets. The compass of our literary development was turning to a temporarily stationary point at a magnetic north in eastern Massachusetts. And, the bloodbath of the Civil War for a time made many gentler things seem trivial, including Irving's idyllic cottage.

Nevertheless, so widespread had been his popularity and so broadcast had been the image of his unique home, that the memory of both lingered on. The property remained in the family across the turn of the century, until in 1945 it was acquired by Sleepy Hollow Restorations, Inc., and shortly opened to the public. Since then one highwater mark in its contemporary history was the official identification by the National Parks Service of the U. S. Department of Interior, in 1965, as a "Registered National Historic Landmark." A bronze plaque has been affixed to a granite marker on the slope above the old villa. It reads in part:

UNDER THE PROVISIONS OF
THE HISTORIC SITES ACT OF AUGUST 21, 1935
THIS SITE POSSESSES EXCEPTIONAL VALUE
IN COMMEMORATING AND ILLUSTRATING
THE HISTORY OF THE UNITED STATES

This modern recognition is important as a sign of continuing interest in this special place as part of our cultural heritage.[50] However, Sunnyside never really ceased to be a Knickerbocker landmark, once it had, under Washington Irving's modest rule, moved from saltbox to snuggery to shrine.

New York: A City of
Constant Change and Accommodation

Jacob Judd

U<small>NSCRUPULOUS</small> political activities have been almost a constant element in city and state elections. While the prerevolutionary days had scattered examples of bribery, nepotism, slander, and vilification, the zenith of such activities is usually associated with the rise of Tammany within New York City. Outstanding as an early organizer of Tammany was the political activist Aaron Burr. It was he who helped create the local political machine which remained dominant until the mid-twentieth century. Burr was a genius at organization who not only established a viable political machine, but introduced electioneering techniques which have remained with us, for better or worse, until the present day. His innovative methods were introduced on a grand scale during the bitter presidential campaign of 1800.

Under Burr's supervision careful plans were laid and carried out as to how the campaign was to be run in New York City. He resorted to what is now a time-worn practice of appealing to the spirit of '76 and to memories of nobler times by trotting out ancient heroes of the Revolution in an effort to dress up his local party ticket.

He organized the city into units and appointed captains responsible for turning out the voters. He went so far as to compile detailed data on each voter which might be used in the effort to sway his vote—a practice bordering on political blackmail.

Both parties hurled invectives and wild charges at each other: The Republicans declared that a Federalist victory would mean the end of American cities, that towns would be burned, and civil liberties would be lost. Republicans, on the other hand, stood for their "talents, their virtues, and their genuine republicanism. They were real Whigs in the days of '76, they were the staunch friends of the revolution."[1]

The Federalists countered by implying that all Federalist officeholders would lose their jobs, veterans' pensions would cease, the navy would be dismantled, farm produce would rot in the fields and in the barns, while laborers would become destitute. According to one writer, the United States, on the day after a Jeffersonian victory, would be "plunged into scenes of horror and misery, similar to those experienced by France . . . which strip man of all that is dear, valuable, and good, and leave him desolate, base and abhorred."[2]

It soon became apparent that patterns established in these early elections carried over into the later period and into other places. Perhaps it was the nature of urban existence which bred a special brand of politics first introduced in New York City. We certainly find such patterns reappearing a half-century later in the third largest city in the United States—Brooklyn—then regarded as a bedroom community of New York City.

The political struggle between Whigs and Jacksonian Democrats of Brooklyn brought with it charges made familiar to us today:

In 1836 the Whigs accused the Democrats of using free-flowing rum to win over gullible Irishmen and floaters, while labeling them as the party of "foreign influence" who had successfully used "corruption and bribery."

Then in 1849 the Whigs were accused of introducing "voters from other wards [to the] exclusion of the proper voters" and to using force to intimidate and keep away opposition votes from the polls.[3] It also became obvious to observers that the public meetings called to ostensibly develop platforms and nominate candidates were "managed" affairs. The Brooklyn Whig organization was admonished for their irresponsible practices regarding these so-called public meetings. If anything, they were not "assemblages for deliberative discussion, and clear sighted and intelligent action," but were regarded as packing schemes by which the party foisted their previously chosen candidates upon an unwary electorate.[4]

In assessing the long-term effects of the American Revolution, the expansion of the electorate as part of a democratization of politics must be regarded as a cardinal result. Once one assumes that more people have the right to participate in the political arena, it then becomes only a matter of time before machinery will develop to involve and to manage such new voters.

Changing political patterns within an urban area can be viewed as an aspect of its growth and development. The populace in general, however, was more concerned with urban living conditions and the problems arising from rapid urbanization. The essentials for living involved obtaining an adequate food supply, decent shelter, sufficient warmth, water for cooking and, occasionally, for sanitary purposes, protection against fire and the protection of one's life and limb. How did the city government cope with such basic needs in an era of expansion?

From the outset, municipal governments did not follow the Jeffersonian precept concerning that government being best that governs the least. Seventeenth-century urban communities were actively involved in supervising many activities. Regulations were adopted concerning the sale and price of bread, bricks, firewood, and, most important of all, alcoholic beverages. Fire prevention in a rudimentary form was observed, and minimal police protection was provided. But municipalities were not involved in supplying water for cooking, in protecting the public's health, nor were they overly concerned with housing. And municipalities certainly were not directly interested in providing such amenities of life as cultural activities and education.

It was in the Knickerbocker era that municipalities, quite often against their will, were dragged into the position where they had to cope with specific problems. New York, for example, did not face up to the problem of acquiring an adequate water supply until it was confronted with two disasters: a cholera epidemic and a massive conflagration.[5]

Education was another area into which municipalities in this

Illuminated scroll containing the memorial resolution by the
Common Council of New York City on the death of Washington
Irving, signed by Mayor Daniel F. Tiemann, December 1859.
In the Library of Sleepy Hollow Restorations. See pp. 120–21
for the text.

IN

COMMON COUNCIL

of the

CITY OF NEW YORK

Alderman

William M. Peck

Presented the following

Preamble and Resolutions which were unanimously Adopted

WHEREAS

His Honor the Mayor has officially communicated to this Board
the melancholy intelligence of the demise of one of New York's
most illustrious sons the

HON. WASHINGTON IRVING

the sad event occurring at his late residence Sunnyside,
on the Banks of the Hudson, in the adjoining county,
on Monday Evening last, at the advanced age of seventy six years, and

WHEREAS

In the decease of our illustrious and honored citizen, it is meet that
the authorities of this the City of his birth should in a becoming
manner evince their sense of the loss sustained by the whole country,
in being deprived of the companionship of one who has by his
exemplary life and his teachings through the medium of his numerous
literary publications tended in a marked degree to elevate the mind,
enlighten the understanding and influence the will of all those of our
citizens who entertain feelings of Love and Veneration for the
cherished laws and institutions of our beloved Country, more
especially in the great and inestimable legacy bequeathed to us in his

Life of Washington
and
Whereas

in the many and important national trusts committed to his charge as
Secretary of Legation at the Court of St. James
and as Minister Potentiary at the Court of Madrid
the energy and fidelity with which he devoted his rare talents and
ability to the best interests of his Country, entitled him to the lasting
gratitude of those for whom he labored and this Common Council,

as the representative of this the greatest commercial, and most important City in the Union feel called upon to pay their feeble tribute of respect to his memory as a public man and

WHEREAS

Possessing as he did in an eminent degree, all those attributes which constitute the scholar the patriot and the statesman his loss will be the more sensibly felt as his death creates a void in the number of our public men, which cannot be filled, in our day and generation; the shining galaxy of noble names, of whom he was a bright particular star having of late years, been gradually fading from our national horizon, never, we fear, to be replaced or renewed by stars of equal brilliancy therefore be it

RESOLVED

That this Common Council, deeply sympathizing with the family of our deceased friend, in their affliction and in consideration of our respect for his memory do recommend that his Honor the Mayor direct the bells in the several fire alarm bell towers to be tolled, between the hours of one and two o'clock on Thursday, December 1, 1859, at which time the funeral will take place from his late residence; that the sextons of the several churches or places of Divine worship, be requested to toll the bells of their respective churches at the above-mentioned time; that the masters of vessels in the harbor the proprietors of Hotels and other public buildings, be requested to display their flags at half mast during the day, and that the flags on the City Hall, and other public buildings, and Institutions of the City, be also displayed at half mast during the day, and be it further

RESOLVED

That the Clerk of the Common Council be directed to cause a copy of the foregoing Preamble and Resolutions to be suitably engrossed and transmitted to the family of the deceased.

Adopted by the Board of Aldermen November 30th 1859.
Adopted by the Board of Councilmen, November 30th, 1859.
Approved by the Mayor, December 31st 1859.

D. T. Valentine, Clerk of C.C.   DanL. F. TIEMANN, Mayor.

Signed

period were drawn quite modestly. The existent eleemosynary improvement societies could not cater to the needs of the city's youngsters, especially those of the working class. Then when politicians latched on to the appeal that public education could have as a device in luring new Irish votes, the inevitable was bound to occur.

While the city began to be involved in such activities, the face and characteristics of the community were undergoing a rapid transformation. It was quite difficult to survive in the city jungle if one happened to be a newly arrived Irishman, a German, or a second- or third-generation black in Washington Irving's New York.

If, however, one belonged to the fortunate few who were above the clamor and filth of the metropolis, then the perspective on Gotham and its problems became a highly modified one.

Washington Irving, born into a middle-class mercantile family, grew up amidst the comforts that wealth and position could provide. Fame came to him early in life while he was in his twenties and he found himself lionized by the society of the day. Then the factors of poor health, family business difficulties, and the urge to see the world combined to send him abroad soon after the close of the War of 1812. He remained in Europe for 17 years and returned as an international celebrity in 1832.

Frequently visiting the city from the time of his return until his death in 1859, Irving constantly remarked about the changing face of the city. He wrote in May 1853, "New York, as usual at this season, is all pulled to pieces, the streets full of rubbish and the hotels full of strangers."[6]

His return to his native land was interrupted in 1842 when he was called upon to serve as the American ambassador to Spain. Again he traveled abroad and with his return to New York in 1846, he viewed the city with a careful eye to detail.

New York is wonderfully improved in late years. A complete new region has been built, and well built. The houses are beautiful and are furnished with great luxury. The tone of society also is greatly improved and the opera house which is

the fashionable assembling place this winter, is giving quite
an air of refinement to the city.

Altogether it is becoming a most agreeable place of residence.
You want to know whether there are not better accommodations to be had than at boarding houses. At present there are
establishments where apartments are to be had on the European plan; where you may have meals in your apartment, and
only pay for what you order. Others are erecting on a large
scale. All these are in the upper and most fashionable part of
the city, near Union Square.[7]

As Irving became more of a suburbanite living in his country
retreat, "Sunnyside," and with old age bringing an increasing
number of physical ailments, the city lost some of its allure for
him. Lamentingly he would write in the last years of his life of a
city he once knew and loved:

New York as you knew it, was a mere corner of the present
huge city and that corner is all changed, pulled to pieces,
burnt down and rebuilt—all but our little native nest in William street, which still retains some of its old features, though
those are daily altering. I can hardly realize that within the
term of my life, this great crowded metropolis, so full of life,
bustle, noise, show and splendor, was a quiet little city of
some fifty or sixty thousand inhabitants. It is really now one
of the most racketing cities in the world and reminds me of
one of the great European cities (Frankfort for instance) in
the time of an annual fair. Here it is a Fair almost all the year
round. For my part I dread the noise and turmoil, and visit it
but now and then, preferring the quiet of my country retreat.[8]

The solitude that Irving so extolled in his little country retreat
is now a thing of the past. The problems of metropolitan living
have exploded into the megalopolis. Some spreaders of doom
predict the demise of New York City as a viable entity while
others assert that the future will bring an amalgamation of the
city with its surrounding suburbs into one huge administrative

entity. The probable course of events will most likely not reach either of these extremes. Rather, New York will continue struggling with its myriad problems and seek accommodations with a rapidly changing world. If anything, the city seems to go through cycles of decline and rebirth. We can truly say today, as did Irving some 120 years ago, that it "is all changed, pulled to pieces, burnt down and rebuilt."

Andrew B. Myers (pages 1–11)

1. "The Knickerbocker Tradition and Washington Irving" was the title of a conference sponsored by Sleepy Hollow Restorations, Inc., in Tarrytown, N. Y., October 28, 1972. The essays in this volume were presented, in somewhat different form, at that conference, which was chaired by the editor. The article on Sunnyside by the editor has been substituted for the interdisciplinary reflections presented at the conference by Professor Donald F. Connors of Fordham University at Lincoln Center, with his gracious approval.

2. Arthur M. Schlesinger, *Paths to the Present* (New York: Macmillan, 1949); revised paperback edition Sentry Edition 36 (Boston: Houghton Mifflin, 1964). Useful as background for this volume is his chapter on "The City in American Civilization."

3. On Porter (1862–1910) and New York, see, for example, Richard O'Connor, *O. Henry: The Legendary Life of William S. Porter* (Garden City, N. Y.: Doubleday, 1970). "A Tempered Wind" is from O. Henry's *The Gentle Grafter* (1908).

4. On Whitman (1819–92), see Gay Wilson Allen's biography *The Solitary Singer* (New York: Macmillan, 1955). The poem referred to here first appeared in the 1860 *Leaves of Grass*. See *Walt Whitman: Leaves of Grass*, ed. Sculley Bradley and Harold W. Blodgett (New York: Norton, 1973), pp. 474–75. The quotation is reprinted by permission. Texts in this paperback Norton Critical Edition derive from the definitive New York University edition.

5. Bayrd Still, *Mirror for Gotham: New York as Seen by Contemporaries from Dutch Days to the Present* (New York: New York University Press, 1956).

6. John Paul Pritchard, *Literary Wise Men of Gotham: Criticism in New York, 1815–1860* (Baton Rouge: Louisiana State University Press, 1963).

7. This title, on a solemn occasion, for many still had the ring of *Knickerbocker Holiday*, the musical comedy by Maxwell Anderson and Kurt Weill, a 1938 success which included in the frolic not only characters from the *History of New York*, but also Washington Irving himself.

8. Thomas Jefferson Wertenbaker, *Father Knickerbacker Rebels* (New York: Charles Scribner's Sons, 1948).

9. The quotation is from Bryant's "A Discourse on the Life, Character And Genius of Washington Irving," a eulogy before the New-York Historical Society, April 3, 1860. See the memorial volume *Washington Irving* (New York: Putnam, 1860), pp. 8–9.

10. Hector St. John de Crèvecoeur, *Letters From An American Farmer*, introd. W. R. Blake (New York: Dutton, 1957), Everyman Paperback

D 8., p. 39. The original edition, some of it written years before, was put out on both sides of the Atlantic in 1782, just as the Revolution had ended.

11. For the quotation in full context, see the Preface by Bridenbaugh to the original edition of *Cities In The Wilderness, The First Century of Urban Life in America, 1625–1742* (1939), available Oxford University Press Galaxy Book 345 (1971). Now a dean of American colonial historians, he followed with an equally important volume, further developing his urban theme, *Cities in Revolt, Urban Life in America, 1743–1776* (1942), paperback edition by Oxford University Press (1970).

12. Kendall B. Taft, ed., *Minor Knickerbockers: Representative Selections, With Introduction, Bibliography, And Notes* (New York: American Book, 1947), pp. xiv–xv, a volume in the American Writers Series edited by Harry Hayden Clark.

13. Perry Miller, *The Raven And The Whale: The War of Words and Wits in the Era of Poe and Melville* (New York: Harcourt Brace, 1956), p. 7. The entire sentence, about the arrival of young Herman Melville (1819–91) on the Knickerbocker scene, reads: "He came as a lamb to the slaughter, with no suspicion that the city of New York was a literary butcher shop."

14. *New York by James Fenimore Cooper, Being an introduction to an unpublished manuscript by the author, entitled The Towns of Manhattan,* privately printed for W. F. Payson in New York in 1930, in a limited edition, with an introduction by Dixon Ryan Fox, p. 16.

15. The 1848 edition by Putnam, which initiated the Author's Revised Edition, is available in numerous nineteenth-century reprints, both in the sets and separate volumes, and is a paperback, Capricorn Books 110 (New York: 1965). For the original 1809 edition the reader is best referred to *Diedrich Knickerbocker's A History Of New York*, ed. Stanley Williams and Tremaine McDowell (New York: Harcourt, Brace, 1927), in the American Authors Series edited by Williams. All earlier versions will be superseded by Michael Black's scholarly edition to be published in the complete Irving Edition by the University of Wisconsin Press.

Michael D'Innocenzo (pages 12–35)

1. Alvin Kass, *Politics in New York State, 1800–1830* (Syracuse: Syracuse University Press, 1965), pp. 133–37.

2. *Providence Patriot,* as quoted in the *Albany Argus,* April 18, 1820.

3. Pierre M. Irving, *The Life and Letters of Washington Irving* (New York: 1863), I, 186–87.

4. Washington Irving, *Salmagundi* (New York: 1904), p. 95.

5. *Ibid.,* pp. 151–52. William Hedges, *Washington Irving: An American Study, 1802–1832* (Baltimore: John Hopkins University Press, 1965),

pp. 58 and 84, is probably correct in his general assessment that Irving did not reveal a gross antirepublican animus. However, Irving's experience in the 1807 election seems to have prompted some of his most cynical views on the people at large. Also see Stanley T. Williams, *The Life of Washington Irving* (New York: Oxford University Press, 1935), I, 94–95.

6. Charles Foote to Ebenezer Foote, March 2, 1807, Ebenezer Foote Papers, New York State Library, Albany (hereafter NYSLA).

7. *Albany Register*, April 17, 1810.

8. Shaw Livermore, *The Twilight of Federalism* (Princeton: Princeton University Press, 1962), pp. 27–29. Although Livermore focuses primarily on the post-1816 period, he suggests that these political practices were absent or disintegrating even earlier.

9. David Hackett Fischer, *The Revolution of American Conservatism* (New York: Harper & Row, 1965), pp. xviii–xix.

10. *Ibid.*, pp. xix, 191–92.

11. See April 1807 entries of Alexander Coventry Diary, 1782–1831 (NYSLA) for meetings of committee of correspondence. For coordinated efforts in different counties, see *New York Evening Post*, April 24, 1807; Henry Livingston to Ebenezer Foote, April 16, 1800, Foote Papers (NYSLA); S. Sherwood to S. A. Law, March 31, 1810, Samuel A. Law Papers, Box I (NYSLA); *Albany Argus*, April 2, 1813, and March 29, 1814.

12. Nominating meetings and formal announcements of candidates sometimes came only a week or two before elections. This resulted in brief campaign periods and undoubtedly placed a primacy on understandings among leaders prior to the formal nominating meetings. *New York Evening Post*, April 21, 1802, and April 15, 1803; *New York Daily Advertiser*, April 10, 13, 1801; *New York American Citizen*, April 11, 13, 17, 1805, and April 5, 1806; Abraham Van Vechten to Ebenezer Foote, March 3, 1807, Foote Papers, Box 5 (NLSLA). However, there were occasional complaints about the exclusion of "the people at large" from the meaningful nomination process. A column addressed to Republican electors in the *New York American Citizen*, April 13, 1805, included this: "NO PRIVATE CIRCLE, NO SECRET MEETING, NOTHING LESS THAN A REGULAR, OPEN, AND PUBLIC ASSEMBLAGE, should ever be permitted to dictate, or even to bias, the choice of representatives." In 1809 and 1810, the same newspaper charged that New York City's "Adopted Citizens" had been excluded from the Republican committee of nomination. Instead of voting for a ticket which "they have kindly nominated for you!" adopted citizens were urged to withhold their votes until they got equal rights in the party. See April 17, 20, 1809; March 27, April 2, 1810.

13. *New York Evening Post*, April 18, 1804; James Oliver to Ebenezer Foote, April 19, 1800, Box 4, Foote Papers (NYSLA).

14. Letter to John Tayler, July 12, 1803, urging that a newspaper be set up to counteract "the mischievous effects" of an opposition press in Washington, Essex, and Clinton counties. Ramsom Collec-

tion (NYSLA); *Albany Argus,* April 6, 27, 1813; New York Evening *Post,* April 21, 1802. Newspapers usually printed only the
names of the candidates they supported. See *New York American
Citizen,* April 24, 1805.

15. C. Elmendorf to E. Foote, April 18, 1800, Box 2, Foote Papers
(NYSLA); E. Foote to Samuel A. Law, March 24, 1810, Box 1, Law
Papers (NYSLA).

16. *New York Gazette and General Advertiser,* May 13, 1800; also "True
Statement of Behren's Case. To our German Countrymen," April
17, 1804, Broadsides, 7799 (NYSLA). For similar Federalist electioneering efforts, see *New York American Citizen,* May 16, 1805.

17. *New York American Citizen,* May 2, 1807. Contrast these statements with Fischer's view that free Negroes were not partisan, *op.
cit.,* pp. 223–24. Also see *New York Evening Post,* April 25, 1807.

18. May 18, 1813.

19. *New York Daily Advertiser,* April 18, 20, 1801; *New York Evening
Post,* April issues for 1803, 1806, 1807, 1810.

20. *New York American Citizen,* April 6, 10, 25, 1807; April 22, 1808.

21. *Ibid.,* April 28, 1807.

22. *Ibid.,* April 11, 1807. Also see April 5, 1806, and especially April 21,
1806: "The plain garb of Republicans don't suit them . . . none but
'Squires' in the Federalist party." "What is the reason that on the
federal assembly ticket there is not a single *Mechanic?* It must be
either that no Mechanic would serve the managers of the party, or
that they hold a Mechanic in too much contempt to nominate even
one of the numerous and respectable class of our citizens."

23. *Evening Post,* May 14, 1806.

24. *Ibid.,* April 25, 26, 1803; April 25, 1807; April 24, 1810.

25. April 27, 1807.

26. *Evening Post,* April 24, 1807.

27. *Ibid.,* April 23, 25, 1803.

28. *Ibid.,* April 20, 1807.

29. *Ibid.,* April 22, 1807, April 22, 1808.

30. *New York American Citizen,* April 25, 26, 1806.

31. *Ibid.,* April 30, 1807.

32. April 29, 1807. Another appeal, almost in identical language, was
made in the next election year, April 21, 1808.

33. *Evening Post,* April 27, 1807.

34. *Ibid.,* April 25, 1807.

35. *American Citizen,* May 4, 1807.

36. See Broadsides 7787, 7798 for 1804 (NYSLA); Amos Douglas to E.
Foote, April 9, 1807, Box 2, Foote Papers, (NYSLA); *American
Citizen and General Advertiser,* April 28, 30, 1800; April issues for
1801. See also *American Citizen,* April 28, 29, 1806, and especially
April 22, 1807, for the plea of "An old Soldier."

37. *American Citizen,* April 28, 1800.

38. *New York Daily Advertiser,* April 28, 1801.

39. *American Citizen,* April 27, 1807.
40. *Ibid.,* April 22, 29, 1807; April 27, 1808; *Evening Post,* April 24, 1807; April 22, 1808.
41. Alexander Coventry Diary, entries for April, 1818 (NYSLA); E. Williams to E. Foote, April 21, 1812, Box 6, Foote Papers (NYSLA); Abraham Van Vechten to E. Foote, March 3, 1807; S. Sherwood to S. A. Law, March 31, 1810, S. A. Law Papers (NYSLA).
42. Fischer, *op. cit.,* p. 95.
43. Asa Emmons to E. Foote, April 2, 1807, Box 2, Foote Papers (NYSLA).
44. *American Citizen,* March 18, 1807.
45. *Albany Argus,* April 13, 1813.
46. As quoted in DeAlva S. Alexander, *A Political History of the State of New York* (New York: 1906), I, 215.
47. "To the Electors of the County of Columbia," Albany Institute Broadside, April 18, 1809 (NYSLA).
48. Broadside 7776, April 24, 1809 (NYSLA).
49. *New-York Gazette,* April 30, 1799; see also *New York Evening Post,* May 15, 1802.
50. *American Citizen,* April 29, 1800.
51. *Evening Post,* April 23, 1803.
52. *Ibid.,* April 24, 1810; also see S. Sherwood to S. A. Law, April 3, 1810, S. A. Law Papers (NYSLA).
53. *American Citizen,* April 29, 1807.
54. *New-York Gazette,* April 25, 1800; *American Citizen,* April 26, 1800; "Bribery, Corruption, Violence and Assaults," Broadside 7792, April 18, 1804 (NYSLA); "Exposure of Federal Meanness and Despotism," Albany Institute Broadside 48, April 27, 1808 (NYSLA); *Evening Post,* April 16, 1805.
55. *American Citizen,* May 2 1807; April 21, 1807. In 1808, a Federalist was charged with offering one dollar to a black man to get his vote, *ibid.,* April 28, 1808. For an example of "treating" in 1806, see McKesson Papers, Box III, New-York Historical Society. On election expenses, see Democratic Party "Election Account Book" (1810) (NYSLA), and Samuel Law to Peter Boyd, April 22, 1810, Box 1, S. A. Law Papers (NYSLA).
56. *American Citizen,* April 28, 1807.
57. *Ibid.,* May 2, 1807.
58. *Evening Post,* May 21, 1807; May 6, 1809.
59. *Ibid.,* May 1, 1807.
60. *Ibid.,* May 22, 1807.
61. Samuel A. Law Papers, April 3, 1810 (NYSLA). See *Albany Register,* April 17, 1810, complaint that Federalists at the last election "brought forward to the polls men utterly destitute of property and supported by public charity who swore that they were possessed of freeholds."

62. Kass, *op. cit.*, pp. 87–88. Also see Chilton Williamson, *American Suffrage from Property to Democracy, 1760–1860* (Princeton: Princeton University Press, 1960), p. 162.

63. Even some of Fischer's "Young Federalists" seem unrestrained in their criticisms of democracy.

64. William Pitt Beers to E. Foote, May 24, 1800, Box 1, Foote Papers (NYSLA).

65. Samuel A. Law Diary, May 17, 1801 (NYSLA); Abraham Van Vechten to E. Foote, May 27, 1800, Box 5, Foote Papers (NYSLA); *Evening Post,* April 28, May 6, 1803, April 19, 1808, and on April 22, 1805, a poem called "Democracy Unveiled."

66. E. Williams to E. Foote, April 17, 1805, Box 6; and Asa Emmons to E. Foote, April 2, 1807, Box 2, Foote Papers (NYSLA). The latter correspondent states that voters have to be led because they are ignorant and prejudiced.

67. Robert W. July, *The Essential New Yorker: Gulian Crommelin Verplanck* (Chapel Hill: University of North Carolina Press, 1951), pp. 19–24. Also see Fischer, *op cit.*, pp. 110–28.

68. *Evening Post,* March 26, 1807; also see *American Citizen,* April 28, 1800.

69. W. Wilson to E. Foote, May 9, 1807, Box 6, Foote Papers (NYSLA).

70. *Evening Post,* March 26, April 20, 1807.

71. *American Citizen,* April 17, 20, 1807.

72. *Ibid.,* May 2, 1807.

73. Richard P. McCormick, "New Perspectives on Jacksonian Politics," *American Historical Review* (January 1960), pp. 299–300.

74. Alfred F. Young, *The Democratic Republicans of New York* (Chapel Hill: University of North Carolina Press, 1967), pp. 576–77.

75. *Albany Argus,* June 11, 1813, discusses the changes of illegal voting in gubernatorial elections.

76. Williamson, *op. cit.*, p. 111.

77. Kass, *op. cit.*, p. 3.

78. Regarding the "explosion of voting" in Massachusetts, see Paul Goodman, *The Decocratic-Republicans of Massachusetts* (Cambridge: 1964), pp. 136–37.

79. Fischer, *op. cit.*, p. 188.

80. For 1820 election results, see John Anthony Casais, "The New York Constitutional Convention of 1821 and Its Aftermath" (Columbia University, Unpublished Ph.D. Thesis, 1967), p. 178.

81. When the gubernatorial suffrage was broadened in 1821, New York voting percentages rose to 58 in 1824 and 54 in 1826, and were higher than those in other Northern states. See Table 3.

82. Richard P. McCormick, "Suffrage Classes and Party Alignments: A Study in Voter Behavior," *Mississippi Valley Historical Review* (December 1959), p. 406.

83. Quoted in Stephen A. Steiner, "Popular Demand for Suffrage Reform in New York State Prior to the Constitutional Convention of

1821" (Columbia University: Unpublished Master's Essay, 1967), p. 14.

84. Quoted in Dixon Ryan Fox, *The Decline of Aristocracy in the Politics of New York* (New York: Harper Torchbook Edition, 1965), p. 234f.

85. *Ibid.*, p. 267.

86. Jabez D. Hammond, *The History of Political Parties in the State of New York* (Cooperstown: 1845), II, 1.

87. *Ibid.*, II, 49.

88. See Steiner, *op. cit.*

89. Carl E. Prince, *New Jersey's Jeffersonian Republicans: The Genesis of an Early Party Machine, 1789–1817* (Chapel Hill: University of North Carolina Press, 1964, 1967), p. 250.

James F. Richardson (pages 36–50)

1. Raymond A. Mohl, *Poverty in New York City, 1783–1825* (New York: Oxford University Press, 1971).

2. For a general history of New York in the last decades of the eighteenth century, see Sidney I. Pomerantz, *New York: An American City, 1783–1803*, 2nd ed. (Port Washington, N. Y.: I. J. Friedman, 1965).

3. Robert G. Albion, *The Rise of New York Port, 1815–1860* (New York: Scribner's, 1939) is an excellent account of New York's maritime development.

4. Charles Rosenberg, *The Cholera Years: The United States in 1832, 1849, and 1866* (Chicago: University of Chicago Press, 1962) provides a graphic account of the state of public health in New York City before the establishment of the Metropolitan Board of Health in 1866.

5. For the motivations of those establishing religious and temperance societies, see Clifford S. Griffin, *Their Brothers' Keepers: Moral Stewardship in the United States, 1800–1865* (New Brunswick, N. J.: Rutgers University Press, 1960); for the benevolent associations and schools see Mohl, *Poverty in New York, op. cit.*, and his article "Poverty, Pauperism, and Social Order in the Preindustrial American City, 1780–1840," *Social Science Quarterly*, LII (March 1972), 934–48. For the police, see James F. Richardson, *The New York Police: Colonial Times to 1901* (New York: Oxford University Press, 1970).

6. The 1855 census figures are from Robert Ernst, *Immigrant Life in New York City, 1825–1863* (New York: King's Crown Press, 1949), p. 193. Ernst's book details the experiences of Irish and German immigrants. For a vivid account of Ireland in the 1840s, see Cecil Woodham–Smith, *The Great Hunger* (New York: Signet Books, 1964). Oscar Handlin, *Boston's Immigrants 1790–1880* (New York: Atheneum, 1968), justly considered a classic, examines the eco-

nomic and social conditions of the Irish in Boston and their cultural clash with the Yankees. See also George M. Potter, *To The Golden Door* (Boston: Little, Brown and Co., 1960).

7. These figures are from statistical appendices in Ernst, *op. cit.*, pp. 200–05. See also *Documents of the Board of Aldermen, New York City*, Vol. 23, No. 16 (1856).

8. The figures on occupations are from Ernst, *op. cit.*, pp. 213–17.

9. George Foster, *New York in Slices: By an Experienced Carver* (New York: W. F. Burgess, 1849). The book, which grew out of a series of articles in the *Tribune*, was published anonymously. See especially pp. 50–53. E. H. Chapin, *Moral Aspects of City Life: A Series of Lectures* (New York: Henry Lyon, 1856), pp. 149–52; E. H. Chapin, *Humanity in the City* (New York: DeWitt & Davenport, 1854), pp. 187–220, examine the slight of and proposes remedies for "The Children of the Poor."

10. For perceptive comments on the personal responsibility engendered by the modern city, see Oscar Handlin, "The Modern City as a Field of Historical Study," reprinted in James F. Richardson, *The American City: Historical Studies* (Waltham, Mass.: Xerox College Publishing, 1972), pp. 17–37.

11. Richardson, *New York Police*, pp. 25–29, 51–53.

12. Sam B. Warner, Jr., *The Private City: Philadelphia in Three Periods of Its Growth* (Philadelphia: University of Pennsylvania Press, 1968) examines the second largest American city rather than the first but similar investigation of New York would show many points of identity with his discussion of the negative effects of "privatism" upon the well-being of the city. On the high costs of limited communication, see Seymour J. Mandelbaum, *Boss Tweed's New York* (New York: John Wiley, 1965).

13. On New York City's housing problems in the nineteenth century, see Roy Lubove, *Progressives and the Slums: Tenement House Reform in New York City, 1890–1917* (Pittsburgh: University of Pittsburgh Press, 1962), pp. 1–48.

14. On these points, see Carroll Smith Rosenberg, *Religion and the Rise of the American City: The New York City Mission Movement, 1812–1870* (Ithaca: Cornell University Press, 1971); Charles Rosenberg, *op. cit.*, part 3.

15. George Rogers Taylor, "The Beginnings of Mass Transportation in Urban America," *The Smithsonian Journal of History* I (Summer 1966), 35–50 and (No. 3, 1966), 31–54. Also reprinted in Richardson, *The American City, op. cit.*, pp. 125–57.

16. Ernst, *op. cit.*, p. 21 for the map and p. 193 for the population distribution by wards. On p. 43 Ernst has a map showing ward boundaries.

17. *Ibid.*, p. 191. For a geographer's account of this process of commercial encroachment upon residential districts, see David Ward, "The Emergence of Central Immigrant Ghettoes in American Cities,

1840–1920," *Annals of the American Association of Geographers,* LVIII (June 1968,), 343–59.

18. Mandelbaum, *op. cit.,* chapters 1–4.

19. *The Diary of George Templeton Strong,* ed. Allen Nevins and Milton H. Thomas, 4 vols. (New York: Macmillan, 1952), II, 56–57, July 7, 1851, 97, June 19, 1852; 369, Nov. 10, 1857; 422, Nov. 20, 1858, are representative entries for Strong's responses to poverty and the poor.

20. For the 1855 census figures, see Ernst, *op. cit.,* p. 193. An important article emphasizing that most immigrants before 1880 did not live in ethnic clusters or "ghettoes" exclusively of one nationality is Sam B. Warner, Jr. and Colin B. Burke, "Cultural Change and the Ghetto," *Journal of Contemporary History,* IV (October 1969), 173–87. A more detailed breakdown of residence on a block basis would no doubt show more residential clustering than the ward figures indicate but I think the essential point still valid.

21. For a general discussion of this point, see Gordon Allport, *The Nature of Prejudice* (Garden City, N. Y.: Doubleday Anchor Books, 1958), pp. 220–23.

22. Ernst, *op. cit.,* pp. 102–11.

23. Richardson, *New York Police,* pp. 129–46.

24. Ernst, *op. cit.,* p. 223. On Tammany and the foreign-born, see Jerome Mushkat, *Tammany: The Evolution of a Political Machine 1789–1865* (Syracuse: Syracuse University Press, 1971), pp. 200–03, 367.

25. A recent study of pre-Civil War nativism can be found in Ira B. Leonard and Robert D. Parmet, *American Nativism, 1830–1860* (New York: Van Nostrand Reinhold Co., 1971).

26. Richardson, *New York Police.* For an excellent study of the political importance of ethnic and religious cleavages in another city, see Michael F. Holt, *Forging a Majority: The Formation of the Republican Party in Pittsburgh, 1848–1860* (New Haven: Yale University Press, 1969).

27. Strong, *Diary, op. cit.,* II, 348, July 7, 1857.

28. Mandelbaum, *op. cit.,* pp. 92–93.

29. Daniel P. Moynihan, "When the Irish Ran New York," *Reporter,* XXIV (June 8, 1961), 32–34.

30. Stephan Thernstrom, "Urbanization, Migration and Social Mobility in late Nineteenth-Century America," reprinted in Alexander B. Callow, Jr., *American Urban History,* 2nd ed. (New York: Oxford University Press, 1973), p. 401.

31. The quotation is from Strong, *Diary, op. cit.,* II, 203, Dec. 27, 1854.

32. Edward Pessen, "The Egalitarian Myth and the American Social Reality: Wealth, Mobility, and Equality in the 'Era of the Common Man,'" *American Historical Review,* LXXVI (October 1971), 989–1034. See especially pp. 1012, 1017, and 1024 for precise figures.

33. Strong, *Diary, op. cit.,* II, 367, Oct. 22, 1857.

34. Pessen, *op. cit.,* pp. 1000–01 on the opulent mode of life of the urban elite.

35. Strong's *Diary,* because of his interest in music, gives a good record of musical performances available to New Yorkers.

36. My friend and colleague Jerome Mushkat allowed me to read his as yet unpublished work on Noah's sketches and reminiscences of the city, which were written in 1849 and 1850.

37. James Sterling Young, *The Washington Community, 1800-1828* (New York: Columbia University Press, 1966).

38. For a sophisticated discussion of the fear of power and the ability to govern, see Mandelbaum, *op. cit.*

Michael L. Black (pages 65–87)

1. Richard Henry Dana, "The Sketch Book of Geoffrey Crayon, Gent.," *North American Review,* IX (September 1819), 348.

2. John Gibson Lockhart, "On the Writings of Charles Brockden Brown and Washington Irving," *Blackwood's Edinburgh Magazine,* VI (February 1820), 561.

3. The letter was written about Oct. 26, 1820, and appears in part in Pierre M. Irving, *The Life and Letters of Washington Irving* (New York: G. P. Putnam, 1864), II, 24–25, hereafter cited as PMI.

4. Washington Irving, *A History of New-York* (New-York: George P. Putnam, 1848), p. xi.

5. This is not the only possible arrangement of the collected works; for example, *Columbus and The Companions of Columbus* could be classified as one of the Spanish works. Three works listed here (*A Tour on the Prairies, Abbotsford,* and *Newstead Abbey*) are included in one volume, *The Crayon Miscellany.* Irving did not authorize the posthumous publication of a reprint of *Salmagundi,* ed. Evert A. Duyckinck (New York: G. P. Putnam, 1860), and *Spanish Papers and Other Miscellanies, Hitherto Unpublished or Uncollected,* ed. Pierre M. Irving (New York: G. P. Putnam, 1866), 2 vols.

6. Irving, *A History of New-York,* p. xiv.

7. Stanley T. Williams, *The Life of Washington Irving* (New York: Oxford University Press, 1935), I, 276 and 459, nn. 155 and 156. William L. Hedges discusses the charges and analyzes a number of the innuendoes in *Washington Irving: An American Study, 1802–1832* (Baltimore: Johns Hopkins University Press, 1965), pp. 192–93, 197–98, 220–23, and 227.

8. Unless noted otherwise, all references to the *History* are to the reprint of the 1809 edition edited by Stanley Williams and Tremaine McDowell as *Diedrich Knickerbocker's "A History of New York"* (New York: Harcourt, Brace and Company, 1927). Because this essay concentrates on the 1809 edition, I have used the spelling *New York* instead of the *New-York* of the 1848 edition.

9. Irving, *History,* pp. 29, 165, 193, 289, and 402, respectively. For the Dutch oath, see C. M. Webster, "Irving's Expurgation of the 1809

History of New York," *American Literature,* IV, No. 3 (November 1932), 293–95; Webster, however, does not explicitly translate "kakkenbedden" ("bed-shitting" in Dutch) on p. 294.

10. *Typee* was first published in Great Britain in 1846, partly to secure the protection of British copyright; when the book was republished in the United States later in the year, Melville agreed to remove some of the offensive and suggestive passages. See Lewis Mumford, *Herman Melville: A Study of His Life and Vision* (New York: Hacourt, Brace & World, 1962), pp. 46–49.

11. See the "uncourteous salute from the watery tail of another comet" (p. 41) and the "display of the graces" (p. 389). Irving even added an indelicate reference to "flatulencies" (p. 393). All references are to the 1848 edition.

12. In the revised editions, none of the examples cited above was expurgated, although some were made less explicit; for example, compare the reference to Swift, p. 29, with the revised passage in the 1812 edition, edited by Edwin T. Bowden (New Haven: College & University Press, 1964), p. 55.

13. Harry Miller Lydenberg, *Irving's Knickerbocker and Some of Its Sources* (New York: New York Public Library, 1953); Williams and McDowell's introduction to the *History,* pp. xliv-l.

14. The best discussion is by Hedges, *op. cit.,* pp. 66–87.

15. The Williams-McDowell reprint is now out of print, but currently available are the Bowden reprint of the 1812 edition and a paperback version of the 1848 edition published by G. P. Putnam's Sons as a Capricorn book.

16. Irving, *A History of New-York,* p. 203.

17. *Ibid.,* pp. 206–12.

18. *Ibid.,* p. 212.

19. *Ibid.,* pp. 228–35; quotation, p. 228. The names of these factions first appear in the 1812 edition; in 1809, Irving used the names *Square head* and *Platter breech* for a discussion of factionalism (pp. 224–28).

20. Irving, *A History of New-York,* pp. 241–48.

21. *Ibid.,* pp. 223–25.

22. On Jan. 22, 1807, Jefferson told Congress that Burr's " 'guilt is placed beyond question,' " Albert J. Beveridge, *The Life of John Marshall* (Boston: Houghton Mifflin Company, 1919), III, 340. He also sent the chief prosecutor a batch of blank pardons which were to be filled in for any Burr accomplice who aided the government, *ibid.,* III, 392–93.

23. Irving, *History,* p. 190. On April 25, 1806, within sight of New Yorkers, the British warship *Leander* fired at the American coastal vessel, the *Richard;* one shot killed the helmsman, John Pierce. From Edward Robb Ellis, *The Epic of New York City* (New York: Coward–McCann, Inc., 1966), pp. 206–07.

24. Not until 1848 did Irving remove the allusion.

25. Jonathan Swift, *Gulliver's Travels,* ed. John F. Ross (New York: Holt, Rinehart and Winston, 1948), pp. 23–24 (in chapter III).

26. *Ibid.*, pp. 33–34 (in chapter IV).
27. *Ibid.*, p. 55 (in chapter VII).
28. Of Jefferson's naval policies, the "gunboats are the best remembered, usually with scorn. . . . They were useful against single vessels in calms, shoals, or cramped channels, and could flee, close-hauled, from any square-rigger, but their only virtue was cheapness." Marshall Smelser, *The Democratic Republic 1801–1815* (New York: Harper & Row, 1968), p. 160.
29. Irving, *History*, p. 207.
30. G. Tremaine McDowell, "General James Wilkinson in *Knickerbocker's History of New York*," *Modern Language Notes*, XLI, No. 6 (June 1926), 353–59. The Von Poffenburgh-Wilkinson parallel had been commented on as early as 1825, notes McDowell (p. 353). See also Williams and McDowell's introduction to the *History*, p. lxvii.
31. Williams, *op. cit.*, I, 98, quoting a letter of June 22, 1807. Two reasons have been given for Irving's presence at the trial: to report for a New York newspaper or "to perform some menial legal functions" (Williams, *op. cit.*, I, 91). Pierre M. Irving is vague on the subject (PMI, I, 190). For Irving as newspaper reporter, see Williams, *op. cit.*, I, 404, n. 141. Since no New York newspaper published anything more than a stenographic report of the trial, Irving's presence was more likely the result of his friendship with William P. Van Ness, a New York judge who had acted as Burr's second in the 1804 duel with Hamilton.
32. T. R. Hay and M. R. Werner, *The Admirable Trumpeter* (Garden City, N. Y.: Doubleday, Doran & Company, 1941), p. 282. This popular biography supplements the more complete biography, James Ripley Jacobs' *Tarnished Warrior: Major-General James Wilkinson* (New York: Macmillan Company, 1937). Hay and Werner recount a number of stories that are not in Jacobs' book, but, unlike Jacobs, they offer no documentation.
33. On Dec. 31, 1807, John Randolph mentioned these allegations and called for a formal court of inquiry; John Chandler of Massachusetts commented, ". . . this was a subject which had long been before the nation. . . ." (*Annals*, 10th Congress, 1st Session, 1257–1269; quotation, 1263). In 1889, Henry Adams offered proof that Wilkinson had been Spanish agent "Number 13" in *History of the United States during the Administrations of Jefferson and Madison* (New York: Antiquarian Press, 1962), III 263. For a brief summary of Wilkinson's Spanish connection, see Smelser, *op. cit.*, p. 112, n. 24.
34. Irving alludes to this in the *History*: ". . . scarcely did the news become public of his deplorable discomfiture at Fort Casimer; than a thousand scurvy rumours were set afloat in New Amsterdam, wherein it was insinuated, that he had in reality a treacherous understanding with the Swedish commander; that he had long been in the practice of privately communicating with the Swedes, together with divers hints about 'secret service money'. . . ." (p. 329).
35. Williams, *op. cit.*, I, 98. Irving wrote this account some days after

Wilkinson had appeared in court. The general wrote Jefferson on June 17 that he had outstared Burr (Beveridge, *op. cit.*, III, 457).

36. Irving quotes two stanzas of "The Ballad of the Dragon of Wantley" in a memorandum book (now at Harvard) and uses them in the *History*, p. 289. He found the poem in Thomas Percy, *Reliques of Ancient English Poetry*, ed. Henry B. Wheatley (New York: Dover, 1966), III, 283–88. The knight is from an unidentified medieval romance (*History*, pp. 291–92). Irving's familiarity with Falstaff was later demonstrated in a sketch, "The Boar's Head Tavern, Eastcheap," in *The Sketch Book;* in the *History*, he refers to Falstaff's description of his regiment (2 *Henry IV*, IV, ii) on p. 301; his journal of Dec. 30, 1804, contains another reference to this character, *Journals* I, ed. Nathalia Wright (Madison: University of Wisconsin Press, 1969), I, 149 and note. For Wilkinson's Sabine campaign, see Hay and Werner, *op. cit.*, pp. 229–32 and 251–52.

37. In the 1848 edition, Irving added an explanation for the general's order: ". . . the general bethought him that, in a country abounding with forests, his soldiers were in constant risk of a like catastrophe . . ." (*A History of New-York*, p. 305).

38. Irving, *History*, pp. 293–94.

39. The best account of the troubles of Col. Butler is in Hay and Werner, *op. cit.*, pp. 229–33. See also Jacobs, *op. cit.*, pp. 199–201. A contemporary account is in Charles William Janson, *The Stranger in America 1793–1806*, ed. Carl S. Driver (New York: The Press of the Pioneers, 1935), pp. 405–411; Janson knew Butler personally and included some of the court-martial documents in his book. McDowell mentions the 1801 order, but not the Butler court-martial, pp. 358–59.

40. Hay and Werner, *op. cit.*, p. 233.

41. J. Thierry Danvers, *Picture of a Republican Magistrate of the New School* (New York: 1808), pp. 15, 20, and 21. McDowell, *op. cit.*, pp. 357–58, refers too broadly to Wilkinson's career in the South in 1806, especially his imposition of martial law on New Orleans (*after* he had "conquered" the enemy forts on the Sabine). Robert S. Osborne criticizes McDowell's choice of New Orleans and concludes, incorrectly, that Von Poffenburgh is not Wilkinson ("Washington Irving's Development as a Man of Letters to 1825," Diss. North Carolina, 1947, pp. 194–95).

42. Von Poffenburgh's story is told in the *History*, pp. 286–311, in Book V, chapter VII and Book VI, chapters I–II. Stuyvesant dismisses him on pp. 327–329, in Book VI, chapter IV. Osborne mentions the general's appearance with Stuyvesant in Book V as an argument against the Von Poffenburgh-Wilkinson parallel (p. 195n).

43. Irving, *History*, pp. 286–88.

44. *Ibid.*, p. 290.

45. Following his source (William Smith, *The History of the Province of New York* [London: John Wilcox, 1757], p. 6), Irving did not know that Kieft had died in 1647 in a shipwreck off the coast of Wales while returning to Holland. In the 1848 revision, Knicker-

bocker finally mentions the shipwreck as part of a story about the discovery of gold in the Catskills (*A History of New-York,* pp. 253–254n).

46. Irving, *History,* pp. 403–04.
47. "Puffing" was used in anti-Jefferson New York newspapers: *People's Friend,* March 11, 1807, and *Post,* November 12, 1807.
48. The first draft is in the Barrett Collection, University of Virginia Library. For Congressional reaction and anxiety about Saratoga from Oct. 7 to Nov. 5, 1777, see E. C. Burnett, ed., *Letters of Members of the Continental Congress* (Washington: Carnegie Institute, 1921), I, 524–45.
49. The story was mentioned during the middle of the Burr trial in the *People's Friend,* July 15, 1807, quoting Dr. Witherspoon. Sam Adams is also given credit for the proposal (Burnett, ed., *op. cit.,* I, 545n).
50. Irving, *History,* p. [lxxxi].
51. "To the Public. The Address of the New-York Historical Society," reprinted in *Collections of the New-York Historical Society, for the Year 1809* (New-York: I Riley, 1811), I, 6. The address was first printed in 1805.
52. Smith, *op. cit.,* pp. 2–10 and 11–23.
53. *Collections,* I, 10–11. Emphasis in the original.
54. G. Chinard, "A Landmark in American Intellectual History: Samuel Miller's *A Brief Retrospect," Princeton University Library Chronicle,* XIV (1952–53), 55–71.
55. One of his notebooks at the New York Public Library is dated "1807–08."
56. PMI, I, 227–33.
57. Irving, *A History of New-York,* pp. xv–xvi. The notice of Knickerbocker's disappearance appeared in both the *Post* on October 26, 27, and 28, and the *American Citizen* on October 27. The traveler's notice appeared in both the *Post* on November 6 and the *American Citizen* on November 7. The prepublication notice appeared in three newspapers: the *Post* on November 29 (not November 28, as printed in 1848), the *American Citizen* on December 4, and the *Commercial Advertiser* on November 29 and 30. The publication notice appeared prematurely on December 4 in the *Commercial Advertiser* but was not repeated; the *American Citizen* of December 6 carried the actual publication notice. All of the newspapers were anti-Jeffersonian.
58. Irving, *History,* ed. Bowden, p. 36.
59. Except for the insertion of some missing letters, Knickerbocker's reply is printed as it appeared, even with the inconsistent spelling of Diedrich's name. The *Republican Watch-Tower,* the country edition of the *American Citizen,* carried the item in its Jan. 26, 1810, issue.
60. In 1842 he had failed twice in his proposals of a revised edition to his publishers Lea and Blanchard of Philadelphia before he left for Spain as American ambassador (letters of Feb. 26 and March 10, 1842, both at Harvard).

Andrew B. Myers (pages 88–115)

1. Evert Duyckinck, "Memoranda Of The Literary Career Of Washington Irving" in *Irvingiana: A Memorial of Washington Irving* (New York: Charles B. Richardson, 1860), p. xv. See p. 86 in this volume for Irving's 1812 report of Diedrich's death.
2. Harold Dean Cater, *Washington Irving & Sunnyside* (Tarrytown: Sleepy Hollow Restorations, 1957), p. 4.
3. Stanley T. Williams, *The Life Of Washington Irving*, 2 vols. (New York: Oxford University Press, 1935), II, 101. Hereinafter STW. Poe wrote this from Philadelphia, Sept. 4, 1838, in a missive to fellow magazinist N. C. Brooks, editor of the *American Museum*.
4. Cater, *op. cit.*, p. 14. The 1656 date may be questioned but is surely a pardonable kind of antiquing by Irving.
5. Pierre M. Irving, *The Life And Letters of Washington Irving*, 4 vols. (New York: Putnam, 1862–64), III, 75. Hereinafter PMI. From a letter to his brother Peter, in France, from New York, July 8, 1835.
6. Joseph T. Butler, *Washington Irving's Sunnyside* (Tarrytown: Sleepy Hollow Restorations, 1968), p. 30.
7. For these quotations see PMI, III, 80, and Butler, *op. cit.*, p. 20, which includes illustrations of Irving's own Gothic designs. On Irving's individual sense of the Gothic, see also Agnes Addison, *Romanticism and The Gothic Revival* (New York: R. R. Smith, 1938), p. 133, and Edward Wagenknecht, *Washington Irving, Moderation Displayed* (New York: Oxford University Press, 1962), p. 44.
8. PMI, III, 92. Whether Astor was on this occasion accompanied by his longtime private secretary Fitz-Greene Halleck is unclear, but this Knickerbocker poet and convivial acquaintance would certainly have been welcome.
9. PMI, III, 116–17. Sixteen years later in a letter to his niece, Mrs. Sarah Storrow, March 28, 1853 (Barrett Collection, Alderman Library, University of Virginia), Irving would write, on hearing of the marriage at Notre Dame of Napoleon III, "Louis Napoleon and Eugenia Montijo, Emperor and Empress of France! one of whom I had as a guest at my cottage on the Hudson—the other whom when a child I had on my knee at Granada."
10. PMI, III, 126. This is an excerpt from an undated letter to his sister Mrs. Catherine Paris. Despite the rebuff, and Irving's well-known distaste for electoral politics, Tammany again considered him for Mayor on his return from Spain in 1846. See STW, II, 361, n. 104.
11. *The Diary Of Philip Hone, 1828–1851*, ed. Allan Nevins (New York: Dodd, Mead, 1936), pp. 423–24.
12. See Washington Irving, *Biographies and Miscellanies*, ed. Pierre Munro Irving, in the Hudson Edition (New York: Putnam, 1866), pp. 501–02, 521.
13. Quotation is from a letter from Washington Irving to Martin Van Buren from "Greenburgh," the township in which Sunnyside lay,

July 2, 1839. Original in the Van Buren Papers, Library of Congress, which include also another invitation to the President in an Irving letter of Feb. 6, 1837. They certainly met later in 1855, for example, at a dinner party in New York City at the invitation of Mayor Fernando Woods, according to an account in *Harper's New Monthly Magazine*. As for Paulding, I have found no record in print placing him at Sunnyside, though it would seem that his intimacy with Irving would have dictated a trip or two. Paulding certainly knew Tarrytown and Irving's neighbors there. See *The Letters of James Kirke Paulding*, ed. Ralph M. Aderman (Madison: University of Wisconsin Press, 1962) esp. pp. 194, 199–200, 275, 287–89.

14. Quotation is from PMI, III, 165. The Berg Collection (New York Public Library) has in its Dickensiana a copy of the *History* from the Gad's Hill library, but with few signs of wear, and regrettably, no glosses. For varying opinions on the Dickens-Irving relationship, see STW, II, 116–17, and Wagenknecht, *op. cit.*, pp. 94–99.

15. Sarah, daughter of Irving's sister Catherine, was extremely close to her uncle. When she moved permanently to Paris with her husband, Irving compensated somewhat for the loss by writing her long letters including minute details of life at the cottage, in Westchester society, and in the city. See *passim, Letters From Sunnyside And Spain, by Washington Irving*, ed. S. T. Williams (New Haven: Yale University Press, 1928).

16. PMI, III, 161.

17. See Andrew Jackson Downing, *Treatise on the Theory And Practise Of Landscape Gardening* (New York: Funk & Wagnalls, 1967), pp. 353–54. This is a modern reprint of the 1859 Sixth Edition, with preface by J. O. Simonds. Downing (1815–45), in the posthumous *The Architecture of Country Houses* (New York: Appleton, 1851), on p. vi wrote, "Rural Architecture is, indeed, so much a sentiment, and so much less a science, than Civil Architecture, that the majority of persons will always build for themselves, and, unconsciously, throw something of their own character into their dwellings." This can be applied directly to Sunnyside. The reference to "the Irving villa" is in a letter from Downing to Alexander J. Davis, a Manhattan architect and collaborator of April 8, 1839 (New-York Historical Society).

18. For this letter to Ebenezer's daughter Sarah, see PMI, III, 276.

19. Prescott first met Irving in New York City in 1842 and corresponded frequently with him. On the 1847 visit, see *The Correspondence of William Hickling Prescott, 1833–1847*, ed. Roger Wolcott (Boston: Massachusetts Historical Society, 1925), p. 635. See also C. Harvey Gardiner, *William Hickling Prescott: A Biography* (Austin: University of Texas Press, 1969), pp. 259–60.

20. PMI, IV, 205. Henry Brevoort died in 1848. On the "Lads of Kilkenny," see STW, I, 76–77.

21. See "Washington Irving In Spain: Unpublished Letters Chiefly to Mrs.

Henry O'Shea, 1844–1854," ed. Clara L. Penney, *Bulletin of the New York Public Library*, Part II (January 1959), p. 25.

22. Quotation is from a Washington Irving letter to Kemble in late spring of 1847, PMI, III, 402–03. The name "pagoda" reflects the touch of *chinoiserie* style in the tower. There may be a Hispanic element too.

23. In his will Irving left Sunnyside to his brother Ebenezer, already an octogenarian. His daughters Catherine (1816–1911) and Sarah (1817–1910) presided over house and grounds almost till century's end.

24. One sign of the high regard Putnam would have for Irving, a personal attachment above and beyond business, is the executive desk he presented to the author with a silver plaque inscribed "To Washington Irving from his publishers, Feb. 27, 1856." It would be placed in the study at Sunnyside, where it remains the most prominent object in the room. See the photo in Butler, *op. cit.,* p. 21.

25. The original of this painting, 8 ft. long by 6 ft. wide, was presented to Sleepy Hollow Restorations in 1953 by John D. Rockefeller, Jr. It is not customarily on view.

26. Fredericka Bremer (1801–65) was in America 1849–51. *America of the Fifties: Letters of Fredericka Bremer,* ed. Adolph B. Benson (New York: American-Scandinavian Foundation, 1924), p. 26. This is a single volume of selections, drawn from the original two-volume *Houses of the New World,* tr. Mary Howitt (New York: Harper, 1853), and reproducing as a frontispiece, along with sketches of Emerson, Longfellow, and Lucretia Mott, her bust of Irving, in left profile, long-nosed and slightly smiling.

27. The original by Lossing, who was a gifted artist as well, is used here as an illustration, on p. 91. For the quotation, and the dressed-up sketch of Sunnyside finally printed, see the two-volume *Pictorial Field-Book of the Revolution* (New York: Harper, 1852), II, 192–94. Lossing again visited Sunnyside "a fortnight before the death of Mr. Irving," who, despite wearying illness, received him hospitably, and bid him adieu with, "I wish you well in all your undertakings. God bless you." Lossing's sketch of the study, "a small, quiet room, lighted by two delicately curtained windows," was included, with his nostalgic account, in his illustrated volume, *The Hudson from the Wilderness to the Sea* (Troy, N. Y.: H. B. Nims & Co., 1866), pp. 343–45.

28. On James, an old European acquaintance, and Irving, in the United States, see PMI, IV, 72–73. James was British consul at Richmond, Virginia (1852–56).

29. Tuckerman's article on "Irving" was a typical piece in Putnam's chauvinistic venture, which included others like C. H. Kirkland's "Bryant," and G. W. Curtis's "Emerson" and "Hawthorne." The 1853 *Homes,* updated with new subjects, but with the Irving piece the same, was republished by Putnam in 1896 as *Little Journeys To The Homes of American Authors,* edited by Elbert Hubbard.

30. Lewis Gaylord Clark, longtime editor of the influential *Knicker-*

bocker monthly in New York City, was an old friend by now. Incidentally, PMI, IV, 419, gives his first name as "Louis." Leutze is Emanuel Leutze, German-born historical painter well received here for patriotic canvases like "Washington Crossing the Delaware." Quotation is from PMI, IV, 103.

31. On the awkward Irving-Cooper relationship, see STW, II, 54–57, 210–11, and James Grossman, *James Fenimore Cooper*, rev. ed. (Stanford: Stanford University Press, 1967), pp. 165–67, 245.

32. *Washington Irving, Commemoration Of The One Hundredth Anniversary* (New York: G. P. Putnam's Sons, 1884), p. 39.

33. See Butler, *op. cit.*, p. 23, in which both portraits, by W. J. Hubard, are reproduced as illustrations. On Kennedy and Irving, see PMI, IV, Index, 431.

34. STW, II, 217.

35. Taylor, a peripatetic journalist, author, and lyceum lecturer, with a high regard for Irving to whom he had dedicated some of his work, wrote in a letter to Philadelphia playwright and poet George H. Boker. See Marie Hansen-Taylor and H. E. Scudder, *Life And Letters of Bayard Taylor*, 2 vols. (Boston: Houghton-Mifflin, 1884), I, 287.

36. *New-York Quarterly*, Vol. IV, pp. 66–83 (quotation from p. 81).

37. *The Letters And Private Papers Of William Makepeace Thackeray*, ed. Gordon N. Ray, 4 vols. (Cambridge: Harvard University Press, 1946), II, 511, 516. Mrs. Proctor was the wife of English author "Barry Cornwall." On Irving and Thackeray, see PMI, IV, Index, 447, and Wagenknecht, *op. cit.*, p. 97.

38. James Grant Wilson, *Thackeray in the United States, 1852-3, 1855-6* (London: Smith, Elder & Co., 1904, reprinted New York: Kraus, 1969), pp. 42–43. Cozzens, a Manhattan wine merchant with a country home in Westchester, was a minor Knickerbocker essayist and humorist, especially popular for *The Sparrowgrass Papers* 1856). The date in Wilson's text is November, 1852," an error for 1855, as Ray (see n. 35 above) points out, II, 510, n. 168.

39. George Pope Morris, editor, poetaster, and playwright, had become a key figure by founding the popular weekly *Mirror*, and was now associated with Willis in the *Home Journal*. Irving used his honorary title as Brigadier General in the state militia. Quoted by permission of the H. W. and A. A. Berg Collection of English and American Literature, The New York Public Library, Astor, Lenox and Tilden Foundations.

40. For the entries of August 19 and 20 including the quotation see George P. Fisher, *Life of Benjamin Silliman*, 2 vols (New York: Scribner, 1866), II, 249–50. On Silliman and Irving, see also J. F. Fulton and E. H. Thomson, *Benjamin Silliman* (New York: Schuman, 1947), pp. 182, 258.

41. The Langenheim picture is in Butler, *op. cit.*, p. 17.

42. See Willis's *Home Journal* piece "Sunnyside in the Summer of 1857," one of two under the heading "Visits To Sunnyside" included (pp. xlvii-1) in the memorial compendium *Irvingiana* (see

n. 1 above). His second piece recounts a last visit late in 1859 in company with J. P. Kennedy. See Henry A. Beers, *Nathaniel Parker Willis* (Boston: Houghton Mifflin, 1899), p. 332, where "Lieutenant Wise, the author of "Los Gringos" is included in the visit. On this final meeting of Oct. 13, 1859, see also PMI, IV, 315, who notes of the trio, "The latter had never met Mr. Irving before, and the others were to see him for the last time."

43. Irving, who had been an executor of Astor's will, was closely engaged in the creation of the public library founded as a bequest. See A. B. Myers, "Washington Irving And The Astor Library," *BNYPL* (June 1968), 378–99, which on p. 397 first prints the formal resolution sent by the Trustees to the Irving family after his death. It is replete with compliments, naturally enough, but these included aspects of his public service to the New York community not unlike those in the Common Council resolution reproduced here pp. 119–21.

44. PMI, IV, 244.

45. Holmes offered his recollections at a special meeting of the Massachusetts Historical Society on Dec. 15, 1859, called to memorialize Irving. Entitled "Dr. Holmes's Remarks," these were printed then (pp. 98–101) as part of Putnam's special commemorative volume *Washington Irving*, actually published in 1860, the spine of which was lettered "Irving Memorial." Quotation is from p. 99. The doctor suggested to Irving both "medicated *cigarettes*," which gave him some relief (p. 100), and as PMI writes (IV, 272), " 'Jonas Whitcomb's Remedy for Asthma' a teaspoonful in a wineglass of water, to be taken every four hours. A good night was the result."

46. PMI, IV, 294–95, notes that on June 13, 1859, Irving received word that the sixteen member Board of Visitors in session at the U. S. Military Academy at West Point wished, if not inconvenient, to cross the Hudson and visit Sunnyside in a body, to render in person "the homage due to one whose long life had been distinguished by sterling virtues, and who wore with becoming gracefulness the laurels which labors successfully devoted to literature had placed on his brow." Though much flattered by these sentiments, Irving, nervous about his condition, hurriedly wrote off, with thanks, to forestall this group arrival, much to the relief of his apprehensive family.

47. PMI, IV, 301–02.

48. PMI, IV, 318–19.

49. See *The Diary of George Templeton Strong*, ed. A. Nevins and M. H. Thomas, 4 vols. (New York: Macmillan, 1952), II, 472.

50. Two other signs can be added. In 1970, during the hundredth anniversary of the founding of the Metropolitan Museum of Art in New York City, one centennial exhibition, dovetailing with a multiform display on "19th Century America," was a major photographic display, directed by Edgar Kaufmann, Jr., on "The Rise of an American Architecture, 1815–1915." Among the carefully chosen exemplars of native styles, in this case in small family houses (rather

than city parks, commercial buildings, etc.) was a striking minimal-size photograph of Sunnyside. In 1973 American Heritage released as an abundantly illustrated two-volume set, a *History of The Artists' and Writers' America,* with the separate volume on *The Writers' America,* in its coverage of Irving, including a color photograph of Sunnyside. This was in fact the only such illustration of a home with literary connections included in the prepublication advertising brochure. The companion *Artists* volume errs, in the Index, p. [409] in stating it was W. J. Bennett who helped Irving design Sunnyside. It was, of course, George Harvey, as the text [134] does make clear.

Jacob Judd (pages 116–124)

1. *Republican Watch-Tower,* April 12; April 23, 1800.
2. New York *Commercial Advertiser,* April 25, 1800.
3. *Brooklyn Evening Star,* May 28, 1836; Dec. 1, 1849.
4. *Ibid.*
5. Nelson Blake, *Water for the Cities* (Syracuse: Syracuse University Press, 1956), pp. 142–43.
6. Washington Irving to Mrs. Sanders Irving, May 26, 1853, Sleepy Hollow Restorations Collections.
7. Washington Irving to Sarah Storrow, Feb. 27, 1848, Yale University Library.
8. Washington Irving to Mrs. Van Wart, n.d. (ca. 1855–59), C. Waller Barrett Collection, University of Virginia.

Ahlstrom, Sydney. *A Religious History Of The American People* (New Haven: Yale University Press, 1972).

The American Heritage History of The Making of the Nation, ed. Ralph K. Andrist et al. (New York: American Heritage, 1968).

Bonomi, Patricia. *A Factious People: Politics and Society in Colonial New York* (New York: Columbia University Press, 1971).

Bridenbaugh, Carl. *Mitre and Sceptre: Transatlantic Faiths, Ideas, Personalities, and Politics* (New York: Oxford University Press, 1962).

Brooks, Van Wyck. *The World of Washington Irving* (New York: Dutton, 1944).

Burr, Nelson R. et al. *A Critical Bibliography of Religion in America*, 5 parts in 2 volumes (Princeton: Princeton University Press, 1961). These two volumes make up Vol. 4 of Smith, James W., and A. Leland Jamison, *Religion in American Life*, 4 vols. (Princeton: Princeton University Press, 1961).

Dunlap, William. *The Diary of William Dunlap, 1766–1839*, ed. Dorothy C. Barck, 3 vols. (New York: New-York Historical Society, 1930).

Dunshee, Kenneth. *As You Pass By* (New York: Hendricks House, 1952).

Ernst, Robert. *Immigrant Life in New York City, 1825–1863* (New York: Kings Crown Press, 1949).

The Heritage Of New York, comp. The New York Community Trust (New York: Fordham University Press, 1970).

Judd, Jacob, and Polishook, Irwin, eds. *Aspects Of Early New York Society And Politics* (Tarrytown, N.Y.: Sleepy Hollow Restorations, 1974).

Mabie, Hamilton. *The Writers of Knickerbocker New York* (New York: The Grolier Club, 1912).

Mitchill, Samuel [By a Gentleman Residing in this City]. *The Picture of New-York; or, The traveler's guide through the commercial metropolis of the United States* (New York: I. Riley, 1807).

Nye, Russel. *The Cultural Life Of The New Nation, 1776–1830* (New York: Harper & Row, 1960).

Pessen, Edward. *Most Uncommon Jacksonians* (Albany, N.Y.: State University of New York Press, 1967).

Pomerantz, Sidney. *New York, An American City, 1783–1803*, 2nd ed. (Port Washington, N.Y.: I. J. Friedman, 1965).

Stokes, I. N. Phelps. *The Iconography Of Manhattan Island, 1498–1909,* 6 vols. (New York: R. H. Dodd, 1918–1929).

Ulmann, Albert. *A Landmark History Of New York* (New York: D. Appleton, 1903).

Washington Irving and His Circle, preface by Stanley T. Williams (New York: M. Knoedler & Co., 1946).

Wilson, James G. ed. *The Memorial History Of The City of New York* 4 vols., illus. (New York: New-York History Company, 1892–1893).

CONTRIBUTORS

MICHAEL L. BLACK is Associate Professor of English at Baruch College of the City University of New York. He is currently preparing Knickerbocker's *History of New York* as part of the Wisconsin edition of the journals, letters, and works of Washington Irving.

JOSEPH L. BLAU is Professor and Director of Graduate Studies in the Department of Religion, Columbia University. He was one of the founders (and several times chairman) of the University Seminar on American Civilization at Columbia; he was also a founder of the Metropolitan New York chapter of the American Studies Association, of which he was twice chairman. His publications include *American Philosophie Addresses, 1700–1900; Social Theories of Jacksonian Democracy; Cornerstones of Religious Freedom in America;* and *Men and Movements in American Philosophy,* as well as a number of articles on themes of American cultural and religious life. Since the early 1950s he has been an active participant in the work of the Committee on the History of Religions of the American Council of Learned Societies, of which he is now chairman.

MICHAEL D'INNOCENZO is Associate Professor of History at Hofstra University. His articles on New York history and the Revolutionary and Civil War eras have appeared in *New York History, The Pan-African Journal, The New-York Historical Society Quarterly, South of the Mountains* (published by The Historical Society of Rockland County), and *The Journal of World Education.* Professor D'Innocenzo received Hofstra's "Distinguished Teaching Award" in 1966. He will be co-director of the 1974 Adelphi-Hofstra summer institute, "New Viewpoints on the American Revolution."

JACOB JUDD is Associate Professor of History at Herbert H. Lehman College of the City University of New York and is the Research Coordinator for Sleepy Hollow Restorations. He is editor (with Irwin H. Polishook) of *Aspects of Early New York Society and Politics.* Professor Judd has contributed numerous articles pertaining to New York history to *The New-York Historical Society Quarterly, New York History,* and *The Journal of Long Island History.*

JAMES F. RICHARDSON is Professor of History and Urban Studies at the University of Akron where he teaches courses in urban and immigration history. A native of New York City, he is the author of *The New York Police, Colonial Times to 1901* and editor of *The American City: Historical Studies* and *The Urban Experience.* He is currently working on a history of politics and public policy in Cleveland in the early twentieth century.

The Editor

ANDREW B. MYERS is Associate Professor of English at the Graduate School at Fordham University. He is also editor of *Washington Irving: A Tribute;* and *The Worlds of Washington Irving 1783–1859: An Anthology Exhibition from the Collections of the New York Public Library.* Professor Myers is editing the Spanish Journals and co-editing *The Alhambra* for the Irving Edition.

INDEX

A

Adams, Henry, 136
Adams, Sam, 138
Addison, Agnes, 139
Adventures of Captain Bonneville,
   The (Irving), 95
Albion, Robert G., 131
Alexander, DeAlva S., 29, 129
Alhambra, The (Irving), 88
Allen, Gay Wilson, 125
Allport, Gordon, 133
Anderson, Maxwell, 125
Astor, John Jacob, 94–95, 109, 139,
   143
Astoria (Irving), 94
Atlantic Cable, 36–37

B

Baker, Ichabod C., 60
Baptists, 52
Beers, Henry A., 143
Beers, William Pitt, 130
Bennett, W. J., 144
Beveridge, Albert J., 135, 137
Black, Michael L., 11, 65–87, 126,
   134, 147
Blake, Nelson, 144
Blau, Joseph L., 10, 51–64, 147
Boabdil, 109
Boker, George H., 142
Bonaparte, Charles Louis Napoleon,
   see Napoleon III
Boyd, Peter, 129
Bradford, Mr., 84
Bremer, Fredericka, 104, 141
Brevoort, Henry, 100, 140
Bridenbaugh, Carl, 6, 126, 145
Brinkersnuff, Christian, 86
Brooklyn, New York, 117
Brooks, N. C., 139
Bryant, William Cullen, 4, 5, 7, 106,
   125
Bucktails, *see* Republicans
Burgoyne, John, 107
Burke, Colin B., 133
Burr, Aaron, 72, 74, 116, 135, 136,
   137, 138
Burwell, Dudley, 60, 61
Butler, Joseph, 94, 139, 141, 142
Butler, Thomas, 75, 78, 137

C

Campaigns, political, 12–35
Carr, Edward, 69
Casais, John Anthony, 29, 130

Cater, Harold D., 93, 139
Central Park, 40
Cervantes, 68
Chandler, John, 136
Chapin, E. H., 132
Charles II, King (England), 68
Cheetham, James, 86
Chinard, G., 138
Cholera epidemics, 41–42, 118
Church of England, 52
Church-state relations, 51–64
Cities in the Wilderness
   (Bridenbaugh), 6, 126
Clark, Lewis Gaylord, 96, 105,
   141–42
Clinton, DeWitt, 27
Cobb, Sanford H., 63
Cole, Charles C., Jr., 64
Columbus, Christopher, 109
Congregationalism, 52
Connors, Donald F., 125
Constant, Anthony, 95
Cooper, Henry S. F., Jr., 5
Cooper, James Fenimore, 7, 8, 106,
   126, 142
Cozzens, Frederick S., 108, 142
Crayon Miscellany, The (Irving), 93
Crèvecoeur, Hector St. John de, 5,
   125
Cross, Whitney R., 63
Currier and Ives, 101
Curtis, G. W., 141

D

Dana, Richard Henry, 65, 134
Danvers, J. Thierry, 137
Davis, Alexander J., 140
Democratic-Republicans, 13, 14, 21,
   26, 29, 33, 34, 35, 71
Democrats, 13, 18, 19, 22, 23, 117
Dickens, Charles, 97–98, 140
D'Innocenzo, Michael, 10, 12–35,
   147
Douglas, Amos, 128
Downing, Andrew Jackson, 98–99,
   140
Draft riots, 45
Dublin, Ireland, 6
"Duke's laws," 52
Dutch Reformed Church, 52
Duyckinck, Evert, 84, 139

E

Education, municipalities and, 118,
   122

149